THINNER DINNERS
in half the time!

BY CAROLE KRUPPA

SURREY BOOKS
230 East Ohio Street
Suite 120
Chicago, Illinois 60611

THINNER DINNERS IN HALF THE TIME is published by
Surrey Books, Inc., 230 E. Ohio St., Suite 120,
Chicago, Illinois 60611. Phone: (312) 751-7330.

This book is manufactured in the U.S.A.

First edition: 1 2 3 4 5

Library of Congress Cataloging-in-Publication Data:

Kruppa, Carole.
    Thinner dinners in half the time / by Carole Kruppa.—1st ed.
      p.   cm.
    Includes index.
    ISBN 0-940625-32-6 : $
    1. Reducing diets—Recipes. I. Title.
    RM222.2.K787 1991
    641.5′635—dc20   91-3721
                                         CIP

Editorial production: *Bookcrafters, Inc., Chicago*
Cover design and art direction: *Hughes & Co., Chicago*
Cover photo: *the National Live Stock and Meat Board*
Typesetting: *Pam Frye Typesetting, Des Plaines, IL*

Single copies may be ordered by sending check or money order
for cover price of book plus $2.50 per book for shipping and
handling to Surrey Books at the above address. The Surrey Books
catalog is also available from the publisher free of charge.

This title is distributed to the trade by Publishers Group West.

This book is dedicated to my husband, Harvey Stern, whose interest and support in my work means the world to me; and to my friends Sharon Askwith and Claudia Beach. To Sharon, I say thank you for your valuable comments and suggestions, and to Claudia, I say thank you for your faith and support when the going got rough.

TABLE OF CONTENTS

1

INTRODUCTION

This book is a collection of delicious, nutritious, economical, quick-and-easy-to-prepare recipes for people who wish to control their weight and enhance their nutrition while enjoying good food. The recipes incorporate scientifically sound nutritional principles with ways to cook food sensibly, a sound alternative to costly diet plans that require a service fee when you join and the continuous purchase of packaged food. These recipes are also family-oriented so you only need to make one meal; those not dieting can eat the same food, just more of it.

Using the cooking technique recommended for each recipe—steam, wok, stockpot, crockpot, baking, and microwave—it is easy to cook several meals at one time and then freeze ahead, making cooking every day obsolete. Almost all of the recipes in this book freeze well and can be reheated easily. The directions for freezing are included with the recipes.

Freezing ahead has many additional advantages for the dieter and health-conscious diner. It allows you to take control of the food you eat. It means you can eliminate loaded-with-sodium-and-preservatives supermarket frozen foods in favor of healthy, low-calorie, low-cholesterol meals that you yourself have prepared. Instead of rushing home from work, too starved to cook and popping something into the microwave or, even worse, sending out for fast food, you can just reach into your freezer and choose a healthful, pre-made meal. The small amount of planning you do each week, or month, can result in dozens of nutritious, ready-to-warm, home-cooked meals.

Some of the recipes in this book call for canned ingredients, which add ease and speed to food preparation. When buying canned products, however, be sure to check labels for sodium and fat content and select items low in these substances. Of course, feel free to substitute fresh products in these recipes for maximum nutritional benefits.

If you are planning a weight-loss program, be sure to see your physician. Your physician can advise you on what your weight should be and how many calories a day you should consume, as well as provide you with information about exercise that should be included in your diet program.

Each recipe in this book includes the number of calories per serving and the quantities of fat, sodium, protein, and cholesterol that it contains. Diabetic exchanges are also given, calculated according to principles developed by the American Diabetes Association.

The recommended cooking method is shown for each recipe, using the following symbols:

| Microwave | Steam | Crockpot | Stockpot |

| Wok | Bake | Gourmet on Wheels |

Now let's take a closer look at each cooking technique.

The Happy Zapper—Microwave Cookery

Microwave cooking is a must for anyone who works, has kids, or plans to do a lot of cooking in a short amount of time. If you don't have one already, and it's the fastest-selling kitchen appliance in America, consider getting one; choose an oven larger than you think you might need. Once you learn to cook with the microwave, you'll use it more and more! Most of the recipes in this book call for cooking on High, or 100 percent, power.

Some ovens have a lazy susan carousel that rotates food for even cooking. If yours doesn't, remember that all recipes must be rotated while cooking to ensure even doneness.

Never use metal containers in the microwave. You may use glass, paper, ceramics, or dishes that specifically say "for microwave use." For multiple-serving recipes in this book, I suggest using an 11″ × 14″ × 2″ dish with curved corners that fits on a carousel and can still turn. It's worth spending money on this one because it's the largest size that can be easily used in a microwave. Bowls or plates that are cracked, chipped, or repaired are dangerous to use in the microwave.

Many of our recipes call for a lid or suitable top over your container to avoid splatters while cooking. You can use paper toweling or microwave-safe plastic wrap over the food surface to prevent this from happening. A cover also will help shorten cooking time.

Read your microwave instruction booklet thoroughly before starting to use your oven. It will not only help ease the transition to this style of cooking but will also help you avoid cooking mishaps and safety problems.

Never operate your oven with the door open; it could result in harmful exposure to microwave energy. Tampering with the safety interlocks is a no-no, too. It is very important that the oven door close properly. If the door is bent, hinges or latches broken or loosened, or door seals and sealing surfaces loose, contact a properly qualified service person for repair. Attempting to fix it yourself or trying to cook under these conditions could result in injury to yourself or others.

Models equipped with automatic temperature controls should not be operated with the temperature probe trapped between the door and the oven front. It's important not to place any object between the oven front face and the door or allow soil or cleaner residue to accumulate on any sealing surfaces.

Microwave Tips:

• Turn the dish when you can't stir the food. Many of our recipes say "give dish a quarter turn," which means to turn the dish so that the part of the food that was facing the sides is now facing back to front. Turning should be done as often as the recipe indicates to assure a perfect outcome.

• The more food you place in the microwave, the more cooking time it will take.

• Some cooking times can be shortened by stirring foods while they're still in the microwave (the walls of plastic-lined ovens don't get hot). Stirring conserves heat.

• Always use potholders when cooking with the microwave oven. Pots get very hot and you could drop one if you're not using potholders.

• Check your dish when the minimum cooking time is up just to be sure you're not overcooking the recipe in your microwave; then continue to cook until done.

• Foods should be spread evenly in the cooking dish for uniformity of doneness. Thin foods such as pork chops, cutlets, etc., cook faster than thick foods such as roasts or whole chickens. Don't stack foods.

• Most meats should be cooked with a sauce. A sauce's moisture causes it to heat more rapidly, and this heat is conducted through the meat, conserving energy and speeding cooking.

• Casseroles should be stirred during cooking. Stirring redistributes the moisture, thus the heat, to each area of the casserole.

• Microwave energy doesn't brown all foods. You can purchase a "browning" dish from your local supplier that will brown foods nicely. You can also use Kitchen Bouquet, Worcestershire sauce, steak or soy sauce, and dry onion soup mix to add a brown color to your food.

Steam Cookery

Although there are many different types of steaming methods, our recipes rely on two:

• A collapsible basket
• A pudding mold

The collapsible basket of interwoven steel or aluminum, with perforated panels that expand to fit several size pans, stands on three legs over water. This versatile and inexpensive piece of equipment should be part of every kitchen.

The pudding mold (casserole; loaf, cake, or bundt pan; or any high-sided, oven-proof ceramic, glass, or metal bowl) is placed inside the steamer on a rack, over water that reaches about two-thirds of the way up its sides. The rack is added to prevent the mold from cracking and to keep it from "dancing" around in the boiling water.

How Food Is Steamed:

Food is steamed by holding it above boiling water. The depth of the water is determined by the height of the rack that holds the food and the length of time needed to steam it. Start timing the cooking when the water in the bottom of the steamer starts to boil and steam is visible. Don't pack foods too tightly in the steamer or they'll take longer to cook.

Steaming Tips:

• Check the water level of the steamer often to prevent burning your pot. Add more water when necessary.

• Wrap the lid of the steamer with a clean, dry towel when steaming uncovered cakes, breads, and some egg dishes to prevent condensation from dripping on the food and making it soggy.

• To set pudding and mousse properly, be sure to keep the steamer covered for a while after the recommended cooking time to allow the food to set properly.

• Leftovers can be reheated by placing the food in the steamer basket, covering with a damp paper towel, and steaming for 10 minutes or until heated through.

Crockpot Cookery

The crockpot was made for working men and women. Arrange your ingredients, turn it on, consult the crockpot chart for cooking time, and walk away. Like magic, you'll have a delicious meal when you return.

Crockpots come in different sizes: 2 quart (for singles); 3½ quart (for families of 4 to 6); and 5 quart (for 6 to 8). A short power-supply cord is provided to reduce the hazards of tripping over a longer cord. All crockpots have stoneware interiors (some have lift-out bowls) that cook foods at a slow pace.

Basically, there are two settings: High and Low. High setting is similar to a 300° oven; Low is equivalent to about 200°. If you plan to cook all day in your crockpot, the Low temperature is recommended. Always cook with the cover on for maximum effectiveness and to prevent facial burns. Cooking times will vary, but I advise you to fill the crockpot at least half full for efficient cooking.

Most vegetables should be cut into small pieces, or at least quartered, and placed near the sides or at the bottom of the pot. Carrots should be covered in liquid. You can make gravy right in the pot. Just add some minute tapioca to any recipe that requires thick gravy. It will thicken as it cooks. Unless you have a pot with a lift-out bowl, storing crockpots with food in them is not recommended.

I own two Rival crockpots that I love. I have had one for about 13 years and the other about 5. I have found them to be very reliable.

Don'ts for the Crockpot:

• Don't add frozen food such as vegetables and shrimp. The stoneware bowl of your crockpot will not withstand the shock of sudden temperature changes.

• Don't use the crockpot for thawing or cooking large frozen foods such as roasts and chicken (unless you first add at least 1 cup of warm liquid).

• Don't submerge the electrical portion of the crockpot in water! Clean your lift-out stoneware bowl right after use with soapy water. Remove persistent stains with Dip-It or a Teflon cleaner.

The Simmering Stockpot

The stockpot is an exception to the classic cooking rule of using only fresh ingredients to make a tasty dish. But the leftovers and food bits and pieces, which the French call *fonds,* or bases, will give you a tasty, low-fat, frugal meal.

Buy a 6- to 10-quart large pot. Stockpots can be made of (classically French) copper, stainless steel, cast iron, aluminum, and enamelware and can range in size from 1 quart to many gallons. The ideal pot is heavy, with a lid that fits securely but lightly on top to allow a small amount of steam to escape. Some lids come with air vents that can be opened or left closed, as needed. Your stockpot can be converted into a steamer by adding an inside rack, steamer basket, or trivet.

Any odd piece of savory scraps, steak, roast drippings, chicken carcasses, bits of fruit or vegetables, roast bones, or steak bones can be tossed into a freezer bag and frozen for use in your stockpot later. They make a wonderful base for vegetable soups, stocks, gravies, etc. Leftover wines can be saved in a jar or bottle to be used in the stockpot.

Don'ts for the Stockpot:

• Don't use the bone or meat of ham or pork. Keep these for use in pea or bean soup.

• Don't add potatoes, potato water, pasta, or rice. These will cloud the stock.

• Don't add creamed vegetables to the stockpot.

• Don't skim stock while it is cooking, but do remove the fat once it has cooled and the fat has congealed on top. Skim the stock if you are planning to use it in aspic or for a clear soup.

A Flash in the Pan—Wok Cookery

The Chinese invented the wok, a unique semispherical frying pan, so long ago that it seems to have always been here. Woks come in sizes from 10 to 32 inches, with covers. Most families require a 14-inch wok, and that size is also best for most of the recipes in this book. The thin round bottom of the wok concentrates heat: It heats up fast and loses heat quickly when removed from the source so foods within will not overcook.

While many purists believe woks are best used on a gas range, I have cooked with one on my electric range for years with satisfying results.

Most woks come with a high, convex cover and a metal ring, or base, that fits on the bottom of the wok, over your heat source. The ring is critical to the stability of the wok and aids in the concentration of heat. On a gas stove, place the ring with the narrow side up, over your largest burner for best results. On an electric range, turn the wide side up. If your wok doesn't come with a deep cover and metal ring, buy them; you'll need them for all of the recipes using wok cooking in this book.

An iron wok is best. Avoid woks with steel and aluminum handles; they get hot too quickly, and you must remember to use potholders.

Woks must be seasoned before use. To season, coat the wok with vegetable oil and place it over high heat. Burn the oil. Repeat this process several times. When the wok bottom is black, it's ready to use.

Get a *siou hok* (a round, ladle-like utensil) and a *wok chan* (a flat turner). The *siou hok* is held in the left hand, the *wok chan* in the right; now stir. The stirring method is similar to tossing a salad and is necessary for achieving a perfect dish. You can substitute a pancake turner and a large spoon if you wish.

In wok cookery, vegetable or peanut oil should be used for best results since these oils tolerate the higher heats necessary. Margarine and butter will burn. Attain a high wok temperature *before adding the oil.* This keeps the food from sticking. Test by adding a scrap of food to the oil. If it sizzles, the oil is ready. You're now ready to start *chow,* or stir-frying!

All vegetables to be stir-fried should be cut uniformly, in small pieces, so they will cook rapidly and evenly. All chopping should be done before starting to cook, and all cooking ingredients should be ready, at wok side, before starting to stir-fry. Ingredients should be organized in the order in which they will be added to the wok. Once cooking starts, things will go rapidly; to ensure a good outcome, all ingredients must be ready in the order needed.

If you are cooking a recipe for a long time, keep the lid on the wok to keep steam out of your kitchen. To avoid hot oil spatters, dry all of your vegetables before chopping and placing them into the wok. Wet vegetable ingredients can cause oil to spatter.

Conventional Baking

You can enjoy baked breads and cakes even if you're watching your weight! You'll find several sensational low-calorie recipes in this book. In addition, below are some baking tips you can use to modify some of your own recipes.

• If a recipe calls for sour cream, try substituting yogurt or buttermilk; you'll eliminate four-fifths of the calories.

• Soy flour can be used to replace up to one-third of the flour in any recipe. The result is a cake a little lower in calories but much richer in proteins than all-purpose flour.

• Use evaporated skim milk instead of heavy cream, and cut calories by three-fourths.

• Use cocoa in place of unsweetened (baking) chocolate. Instead of 1 ounce of solid chocolate (143 calories), use 3 tablespoons unsweetened cocoa (60 calories). You can also use chocolate extract (much lower in calories) in many recipes and still enjoy a good chocolate flavor.

• Substitute 2 egg whites for each whole egg called for in the recipe.

• Sugar substitutes can be a big help when creating cake and pie recipes. You can even use a combination of sugar plus a substitute to lower the calories.

• If you need to thicken a fruit pie filling, use cornstarch instead of flour. Even though they both have 29 calories per tablespoon, you will only need half as much.

• Spices add so much to a pie—except calories—you're wise to add them for taste. A touch of vanilla can heighten the impression of sweetness, and extracts such as orange are terrific flavor enhancers.

Gourmet on Wheels

I have coined the term "Gourmet on Wheels" to indicate recipes that require little or no cooking. Instead, they rely on items picked up at the deli counter, frozen foods, pasta with no-cook sauces, and other prepared items. Of course, such meals do not have to be unimaginative or simply "store-bought." They may easily be adorned with personal touches that belie the fact that they were created in minutes.

For example, you can add a sauce to a deli chicken, stir-fry fresh vegetables from the salad bar, and add Grand Marnier to fresh fruit salad for an almost instant meal. You may be surprised to learn that you can now buy instant brown rice, microwave pasta, and canned bean salads that only need the addition of a herb or two to be complete.

Choose and keep staples you love—such as canned mushrooms, olives, artichoke hearts, or roasted peppers—in your pantry so you'll be ready to dress up a simple meal. Also, use your freezer to help create wonderful meals in record time. Frozen vegetables and stock are the beginnings of a great soup. Add tortellini and you have a hearty main dish. Always keep a selection of herbs on hand so you can create customized touches with little work, such as a dill sauce for frozen fish. No-cook or quick-to-cook pasta sauces will allow you to serve dinner with speed and élan.

Freezing Tips

Almost all of the recipes in this book can be frozen. By preparing foods ahead and freezing them in the portions you need, you'll have a veritable supermarket of choices immediately available when you need them! Freezing and reheating directions are given with the recipes; but here are some general tips to ensure good results.

• Choose only the best, top-quality ingredients for cooking and freezing; that will assure the best nutrition and flavor.

• For safety's sake, cool all recipes quickly and freeze promptly. A recipe that's allowed to stand a day or two before freezing will not have peak freshness and flavor.

• Leave room at the top of all freezer bags or containers, as liquids will expand after they are unfrozen.

• Do not refreeze any food. Refreezing will allow spoilage, and foods will lose their taste and flavor, not to mention many of their nutrients.

• Use good quality materials for freezing. I recommend sealing foods in moisture-resistant, vacuum-sealed bags.

• Freezer wraps, containers such as those made by Tupperware, Rubbermaid, etc., or a vacuum sealing machine, such as the one made for home use by Deni, all can be used. Regular plastic wrap is not recommended for freezer items.

• All food items should be wrapped securely with minimum air, vapors, or moisture trapped in the bags or wraps.

• Items frozen in individual portions are best when vacuum sealed for boil-in-the-bag reheating.

• Foods that are not sealed in the boil-in-the-bag method should be thawed in the refrigerator in their original containers prior to heating and serving. Or they may be reheated in the microwave. Then, be sure the items are in microwave-safe containers.

• Write the date, contents of package, and number of servings on each freezer bag, wrap, or container to avoid confusion.

• Store all frozen foods at a temperature of 0° F or lower for safe freezing.

• For maximum flavor and freshness retention, rotate your freezer foods so they don't exceed the expiration dates.

• Consult a freezer storage chart to see what the maximum expiration dates are for certain types of foods and recipes.

• If freezer temperature is allowed to rise above 25° or 30° F, or if freezer has been turned off for any period of time, it will affect the nutrient value and safety of your recipes.

Vacuum Sealing Machines

Today's vacuum sealing machines are extremely easy to operate. Get one designed for home use. They are the safest way to seal bags for freezing and require only a three-step method:

- Make the bag
- Vacuum seal
- Place a second, final, seal on the bag

That's all there is to it! Boil-in-the-bag foods retain their flavor better, cooking odors are reduced, your saucepan remains cleaner, and you save fuel.

By removing most of the air, vapors, and moisture from the bag, your foods are frozen more safely, retain longer shelf life, and retain natural flavors and colors longer. Follow the instructions of the vacuum sealing machine's manufacturer to the letter.

Vacuum Sealing Tips:

- To get a perfect seal, make sure there are no creases or wrinkles in the film, and the area to be sealed is clean and dry.
- Leave a 1½-inch margin between the food and the seal to allow for freezing and cooking expansion of the foods.
- Label all foods on the white strips on the bags.
- Foods should be cooled, sealed, and frozen promptly for peak flavor.
- Reduce some seasonings and flavorings in recipes, according to your taste, because they will intensify when frozen.
- Don't use cling-type film with a bag sealer; the heat of the sealing process will melt the film.
- Don't use vacuum air extraction when sealing liquids in bags.
- If particles of film adhere to the sealing wire, wipe them off to prevent damage to the wire.
- Remove the cord plug from the socket before trying to clean your machine.
- Don't use abrasive cleaners, and never submerge your machine in water.
- Wipe the casing with a soft, damp cloth only.

2

SLIM STARTERS

Classic Eggplant Caponata

Eggplant cooked in the microwave retains a beautiful green color instead of becoming dull brown like roasted eggplant. It is quite appealing.

1 large eggplant (about 1 lb.), pricked with a fork

1 onion, peeled and chopped (about ½ cup)
¼ cup parsley, chopped
1 clove garlic, minced
2 tablespoons capers
1 teaspoon basil
1 teaspoon oregano
¼ cup black olives, sliced
2 tablespoons olive oil
2 teaspoons fresh lemon juice

Makes 2 cups of dip.
Serves 32.

Place eggplant on a double thickness of paper toweling and microwave, uncovered, on High 12 minutes. Set aside to cool.

In a food processor, add onion, parsley, garlic, capers, basil, oregano, and olives and process till just mixed. Cut eggplant in half lengthwise and scoop out flesh. Add flesh to contents in food processor, and process just until mixture is coarsely chopped. Transfer to serving bowl. Stir in oil and lemon juice.

Serve at room temperature with pita bread, crackers, or raw vegetables.

To Freeze: Vacuum seal 1 cup in a bag; label and freeze for up to 2 months.

To Serve: Thaw in refrigerator. Serve at room temperature with pita bread or raw vegetables.

Per Serving:		Diabetic Exchanges per Serving:	
calories:	11	milk:	0
protein (gm):	0.1	vegetable:	0
fat (gm):	1.0	fruit:	0
cholesterol (mg):	0	bread:	0
sodium (mg):	5	meat:	0
		fat:	0

Antipasto

Dressing:
2 tablespoons plus 2
 teaspoons olive oil
2 tablespoons onion, diced
1 tablespoon red wine vinegar
1 tablespoon lemon juice
1 tablespoon chives, minced
1 garlic clove, minced
¼ teaspoon basil
¼ teaspoon oregano

Vegetables:
2 cups cauliflower florets,
 blanched or raw

24 asparagus spears, cooked
1 (15½-oz.) can artichoke
 hearts
1 large red onion, sliced and
 separated into rings
6 ozs. drained chickpeas
8 cherry tomatoes, cut in half
Several large lettuce leaves for
 platter
½ cup part-skim mozzarella
 cheese, shredded
¼ cup black olives, sliced

Serves 4.

To Prepare Dressing: In small bowl, combine all ingredients for dressing; set aside.

To Prepare Marinated Vegetable Mixture: In large bowl, combine cauliflower, asparagus, artichoke hearts, onion, chickpeas, and tomatoes. Pour dressing over vegetable mixture and toss to coat. Cover and refrigerate for at least 1 hour, tossing several times.

To Serve: Line large serving platter with lettuce. Spoon vegetable mixture into center of platter. Top with vegetables. Sprinkle with mozzarella cheese and olives.

Note: It is not recommended that you freeze this dish. Serve it fresh.

Per Serving:		Diabetic Exchanges per Serving:	
calories:	314	milk:	0
protein (gm):	16.3	vegetable:	5
fat (gm):	16.1	fruit:	0
cholesterol (mg):	16	bread:	0
sodium (mg):	414	meat:	1
		fat:	3

Marinated Mushrooms

⅔ cup balsamic vinegar
⅓ cup olive oil
2 tablespoons granulated sugar
1 teaspoon dried basil
1 teaspoon dried thyme
1 teaspoon dried oregano
2 tablespoons water
Freshly ground pepper
1 medium red onion, sliced
1½ lbs. medium mushrooms
½ cup chives, minced
Serves 10.

In large bowl, combine vinegar, oil, sugar, basil, thyme, oregano, water, and pepper. Stir until well mixed.

Separate onion into rings. Rinse mushrooms and trim stems. Add mushrooms and onion to vinegar mixture; mix lightly. Cover and refrigerate for at least 8 hours, stirring occasionally. Drain before serving. Place on platter with toothpicks; garnish with chives.

Variation: Add artichoke hearts, hearts of palm, or asparagus to the mushrooms for a different salad.

Note: This can be used as a first course by serving on a bed of interesting greens such as romaine, Boston lettuce, or arugula.

To Freeze: Place in vacuum-sealed bags; label and freeze for up to 2 months.

To Serve: Thaw in refrigerator and serve cold.

Per Serving:		Diabetic Exchanges per Serving:	
calories:	96	milk:	0
protein (gm):	1.6	vegetable:	1
fat (gm):	7.5	fruit:	0
cholesterol (mg):	0	bread:	0
sodium (mg):	2	meat:	0
		fat:	1½

Marinated Tortellini Vegetable Kabobs

⅔ cup water
½ cup wine or cider vinegar
1 teaspoon dried basil
1 teaspoon oregano
½ teaspoon dry mustard
½ teaspoon thyme
1 teaspoon Spike
¼ teaspoon pepper, freshly ground
½ teaspoon dill
¼ teaspoon onion powder
¼ teaspoon garlic powder
24 cooked small fresh spinach tortellini with cheese; or 24 cheese tortellini; or 48 tricolored tortellini
1 cup button mushrooms (about 12)
6 artichoke hearts, cut into quarters
12 cherry tomatoes, halved
24 (6-inch) skewers
Makes 24 appetizers.
Serves 12.

Combine first 11 ingredients in a saucepan; gradually bring to a boil. Cook 30 seconds, stirring with a wire whisk. Remove from heat and let cool.

Alternate tortellini, mushrooms, artichokes, and tomatoes on skewers; place in a 13 × 9 × 2-inch baking dish. Pour dressing over kabobs, turning to coat. Cover and marinate in refrigerator 4 hours, turning occasionally. Drain and place on a serving platter.

Note: Only the tortellini and dressing should be frozen as follows.

To Freeze: Vacuum seal tortellini and dressing; label, and freeze for up to 2 months.

To Serve: Thaw, add remaining vegetables to marinate, and complete the kabobs.

Per Serving:		Diabetic Exchanges per Serving:	
calories:	79	milk:	0
protein (gm):	3.2	vegetable:	1
fat (gm):	1.2	fruit:	0
cholesterol (mg):	0	bread:	½
sodium (mg):	289	meat:	½
		fat:	0

Mediterranean Artichoke Dip

1 (14-oz.) can artichoke hearts, drained and coarsely chopped
1 tablespoon pimiento, diced
1 tablespoon green bell pepper, diced
1 tablespoon reduced-calorie mayonnaise
2 teaspoons grated Parmesan cheese
1 teaspoon lemon juice
1 teaspoon dried oregano
1 teaspoon dried basil
¼ teaspoon garlic powder
¼ teaspoon hot sauce (optional)

Makes 1⅓ cups.
Serves 6.

Combine all ingredients in a bowl; stir well. Cover and chill well. Serve with crisp bread or plain crackers.

To Freeze: Vacuum seal, label, and freeze for up to 2 months.

To Serve: Thaw in refrigerator and serve well chilled with crackers.

Per Serving:		Diabetic Exchanges per Serving:	
calories:	40	milk:	0
protein (gm):	1.7	vegetable:	1
fat (gm):	1.0	fruit:	0
cholesterol (mg):	1	bread:	0
sodium (mg):	51	meat:	0
		fat:	½

Salmon Ball

1 15½-oz. can salmon
1 tablespoon lemon juice
1 tablespoon horseradish
8 ozs. plain low-fat yogurt

1 tablespoon dill
4 green onions, chopped
½ cup parsley, chopped
Cucumber slices and celery
  sticks
Serves 10.

Drain salmon and flake with fork into bowl. Mix in all other ingredients except parsley, cucumber slices, and celery. Shape into ball and roll in parsley flakes. Place on plate surrounded by cucumber slices and celery. Do not freeze this dish.

Per Serving:		**Diabetic Exchanges per Serving:**	
calories:	77	milk:	0
protein (gm):	10.0	vegetable:	0
fat (gm):	3.0	fruit:	0
cholesterol (mg):	1	bread:	0
sodium (mg):	277	meat:	1½
		fat:	0

Shrimp Cocktail Supreme

1 lb. Poached Shrimp (see p. 123)

1 recipe Zesty Cocktail Sauce (see p. 165)
1 green bell pepper
Serves 6.

Mound shrimp in a shallow dish filled with ice. Place cocktail sauce in a hollowed-out green pepper placed in center of shrimp.

To Freeze: Vacuum seal shrimp and cocktail sauce in individual bags, label, and freeze for up to 2 months.

To Serve: Thaw in refrigerator.

Per Serving:		Diabetic Exchanges per Serving:	
calories:	119	milk:	0
protein (gm):	16.4	vegetable:	0
fat (gm):	0.8	fruit:	0
cholesterol (mg):	148	bread:	0
sodium (mg):	713	meat:	2
		fat:	0

Mexican Popcorn

7 cups air-popped popcorn

Vegetable cooking spray
Mexican seasoning
Serves 8.

Spray popcorn with vegetable cooking spray. (This helps to keep seasoning on popcorn.) Sprinkle with Mexican seasoning to taste.

Per Serving:		Diabetic Exchanges per Serving:	
calories:	21	milk:	0
protein (gm):	0.8	vegetable:	0
fat (gm):	0.0	fruit:	0
cholesterol (mg):	0	bread:	½
sodium (mg):	0	meat:	0
		fat:	0

Spicy Popcorn Schnibble

7 cups air-popped popcorn
1 cup tiny salted pretzels
1 tablespoon vegetable oil

1½ teaspoons salt-free herb
  and spice blend
½ teaspoon Spike
¼ teaspoon garlic powder
1 teaspoon fresh parsley,
  minced

Makes about 8 cups.
Serves 8.

Combine first 2 ingredients in bowl; drizzle with oil. Combine remaining ingredients and sprinkle over popcorn mixture; toss well. Spread mixture in 15×10×1-inch jellyroll pan. Bake at 350° for 20 minutes; stir once. Turn oven off; let cool in oven. Store in airtight container.

Per Serving:		Diabetic Exchanges per Serving:	
calories:	37	milk:	0
protein (gm):	0.8	vegetable:	0
fat (gm):	1.7	fruit:	0
cholesterol (mg):	0	bread:	½
sodium (mg):	1	meat:	0
		fat:	0

Yogurt Cheese

This cheese resembles a boursin (creamy French cheese) and is often mixed with garlic and herbs. You can try this recipe or experiment with one of your own. Try other herbs such as cilantro or dill. You can also add chilies if you like.

4 cups plain low-fat yogurt
1 clove garlic, finely minced
2 tablespoons fresh parsley, minced
1 teaspoon each minced thyme, oregano, and tarragon
½ teaspoon Spike or to taste
Makes 2 cups.
Serves 16.

Rinse a long length of cheesecloth (about 1 ft.) in cold water and wring out. Place yogurt in center, wrap cloth around it, and place in strainer or colander in a bowl. Refrigerate until thick, 8 to 14 hours or up to 24 hours. Discard whey (the separated liquid), and unwrap yogurt cheese. Place in mixing bowl and mix thoroughly with garlic, parsley, herbs, and Spike. Serve with crackers or fresh vegetables.

To Freeze: Place in freezer container; label and freeze for up to 2 months.

To Serve: Thaw in refrigerator, then serve.

Per Serving:		Diabetic Exchanges per Serving:	
calories:	29	milk:	½
protein (gm):	2.7	vegetable:	½
fat (gm):	0.8	fruit:	0
cholesterol (mg):	3	bread:	0
sodium (mg):	25	meat:	0
		fat:	0

3

THE EARL OF SANDWICH

Versatility is what makes the sandwich so popular today. You can make large sandwiches such as heroes or small dainty tea sandwiches. While a sandwich is the meal of choice for lunch in this country, a sandwich is just as at home for breakfast or supper.

Today we have an endless list of special breads to choose among when making sandwiches. Among the newest innovations are the lower-calorie breads, containing only 40 calories, that have recently come on the market. These offer a great diet alternative, and they taste great. Since pita bread has become so popular today, and many of you may have difficulty finding it in your locale, I have included a recipe since I believe once you make your own pita, you will never buy it again.

About Mustard

Americans love mustard, and each year new flavors appear on store shelves. While many are imported, several small American companies are producing some of the best-flavored mustards available anywhere. I think your pantry should stock at least four different mustards. First, you will need a Dijon, and next I would choose a honey mustard. Other choices could be a fruit-flavored mustard, such as cranberry, or cherry mustard. Another choice would be a French mustard, Bordeaux, a sweet-sour type. You can also find mustards flavored with Provencal herbs and tarragon. Dusseldorf is the best known of the German mustards, for those who like a mildly spiced, smooth mustard.

About Mayonnaise

Reduced-calorie mayonnaise has half the fat and calories of the regular and tastes just as good. However, it still gets nearly 100 percent of its calories from fat. A better choice would be Miracle Whip Light Salad Dressing, which will beat that percentage. Try it and see if you can switch.

Basic Tips

• Always read the recipe at least twice before you begin cooking.

• Add additional seasonings such as herbs or spices after you have tasted the dish.

• Most recipes in this book can be halved or doubled successfully.

• Put something between the bread and the spread (mayonnaise or mustard) such as a lettuce leaf so the sandwich will not become soggy.

• If you are taking sandwiches on a picnic or to work, pack the tomatoes, cucumbers, and other moist items separately from the bread. You will have a fresher sandwich if you assemble it just before you are going to eat it.

Pan Bagna

This is a staple French sandwich sold in the streets everywhere in France. You can vary the fillings, but I like this one the best.

1 can (6½ ozs.) tuna in spring water
1 tablespoon olive oil
2 tablespoons red wine vinegar
¼ teaspoon garlic, minced

One large loaf Italian bread, cut in half with insides scooped out
1 jar (7 ozs.) roasted red peppers, drained
5 radishes, sliced thin
1 cucumber, sliced thin
1 tomato, sliced thin
3 scallions, sliced thin
¼ cup fresh basil, chopped
Serves 6.

Drain water from tuna and set aside. In a bowl, combine oil, vinegar, and garlic. Whisk to blend. Spoon dressing over both sides of the bread. Place bread on a large plate. Spoon tuna evenly over one side of bread. Top with one layer each roasted peppers, radishes, cucumber, tomato, scallions, and basil. Cover with other side of bread. Wrap loaf in plastic wrap. Place on plate and refrigerate. To serve, let stand at room temperature for 30 minutes. Unwrap and cut into 6 pieces.

To Freeze: Mix filling ingredients and vacuum seal individual portions; label and freeze for up to 2 months.

To Serve: Thaw filling. Make dressing and spread on bread. Spoon filling into sandwich. Wrap loaf in plastic wrap and refrigerate. Let stand 30 minutes at room temperature before serving. Cut into 6 pieces.

Per Serving:		Diabetic Exchanges per Serving:	
calories:	249	milk:	0
protein (gm):	14.3	vegetable:	1
fat (gm):	3.2	fruit:	0
cholesterol (mg):	11	bread:	2
sodium (mg):	419	meat:	1
		fat:	½

Teriyaki Sandwiches

2 to 2½ lbs. boneless beef chuck steak
¼ cup low-sodium soy sauce
1 tablespoon brown sugar
1 clove garlic, minced
4 teaspoons arrowroot

2 tablespoons water
1 cup mushrooms, sliced
8 pita breads, split in half
Garnishes: split cherry tomatoes, chopped green onion, sprouts, or shredded lettuce

Serves 8.

Cut steak into thin 2-in. pieces. Combine soy sauce, brown sugar, and garlic. Stir in meat. Put meat into 3⅓- to 4-quart crockpot. Cover; cook on Low 7 to 9 hours, or High 3 to 4 hours. Remove meat from cooking juices.

Measure 1½ cups cooking juices (add water if necessary) and place in saucepan. Combine arrowroot and 2 tablespoons water, add mushrooms, and place in pan. Cook and stir till thickened and bubbly. Stir in cooked meat. Heat through. (You can freeze at this point or serve.)

To Serve Immediately: Spoon beef into pita halves. Place 2 halves on each plate and add garnishes.

To Freeze: Vacuum seal individual portions; label and freeze for up to 2 months.

To Reheat: Put bags in boiling water, and bring to a boil again. Boil 10 to 12 minutes.

Per Serving:		Diabetic Exchanges per Serving:	
calories:	303	milk:	0
protein (gm):	16.6	vegetable:	0
fat (gm):	6.0	fruit:	0
cholesterol (mg):	28	bread:	3
sodium (mg):	525	meat:	1
		fat:	1

Chicken Salad Deluxe Sandwich

3 cups cooked or canned chicken, cubed
1½ cups celery, sliced
¼ cup scallions, sliced
½ cup low-fat yogurt

¼ cup light sour cream
1½ teaspoons dried tarragon
2 tablespoons chives, chopped
Freshly ground pepper
12 slices reduced-calorie Italian bread
Lettuce leaves

Serves 6.

In a large bowl, combine chicken, celery, scallions, yogurt, sour cream, tarragon, and chives. Mix lightly. Before serving, season with pepper to taste. Spoon chicken salad onto each of 6 pieces of bread. Top with a lettuce leaf. Cover with second slice of bread and cut in half to serve.

To Freeze: Vacuum seal individual portions of filling; label and freeze for up to 2 months.

To Serve: Thaw in refrigerator, toss well, and spoon filling into sandwich.

Per Serving:		Diabetic Exchanges per Serving:	
calories:	214	milk:	0
protein (gm):	22.2	vegetable:	0
fat (gm):	3.9	fruit:	0
cholesterol (mg):	49	bread:	1
sodium (mg):	243	meat:	2
		fat:	1

French Bread Pizzas

¼ lb. ground chuck
¼ lb. ground turkey
¼ cup green bell pepper, chopped
¼ cup onion, chopped
1 tablespoon garlic powder
1 cup marinara sauce
2 cups mushrooms, sliced
1 teaspoon dried oregano
1 (1-lb.) loaf French bread
¼ cup (2 ozs.) shredded part-skim mozzarella cheese
Serves 8.

Break up ground beef and turkey in very small chunks in 2-qt. casserole. Add green pepper, onion, and garlic powder. Place in microwave oven. Cook 5 to 7 minutes, stirring about every 2 minutes. Add marinara sauce, mushrooms, and oregano and microwave another 4 minutes.

Slice bread in half lengthwise; place cut sides up on baking sheet. Spread meat mixture evenly over bread. Top with mozzarella cheese. Microwave 2 minutes or until cheese melts.

To Freeze: Place in microwave-safe casserole; label and freeze for up to 2 months.

To Serve: Thaw. Cover with microwave-safe plastic wrap, and cook on High for 3 to 5 minutes.

Per Serving:		Diabetic Exchanges per Serving:	
calories:	257	milk:	0
protein (gm):	13.8	vegetable:	1
fat (gm):	7.7	fruit:	0
cholesterol (mg):	23	bread:	2
sodium (mg):	563	meat:	1
		fat:	1

Vegetarian Pizzas

Vegetable cooking spray
3 tablespoons Bermuda onion,
  chopped
1 clove garlic, minced
½ cup fresh mushrooms, sliced
½ cup sun-dried tomatoes
⅓ cup carrot, coarsely shredded
¼ cup red, green, or yellow
  bell peppers, chopped

1 tablespoon fresh cilantro,
  minced
2 (6-in.) flour tortillas
¾ cup (3 ozs.) shredded part-
  skim mozzarella cheese,
  divided
½ cup canned kidney beans,
  drained
Serves 2.

Coat a medium non-stick skillet with cooking spray; place over medium heat until hot. Add onion and garlic; saute 1 minute. Add mushrooms, tomatoes, and carrot; saute 2 minutes. Add peppers and saute 2 more minutes. Stir in cilantro; set aside.

Place tortillas on a baking sheet and broil 6 in. from heat 2 minutes. Turn tortillas over; broil 1 minute or until crisp. Remove from oven. Top each tortilla with ¼ cup plus 1 tablespoon cheese, ¼ cup beans, half of vegetable mixture, and 1 tablespoon remaining cheese. Broil 6 in. from heat 1 minute or until cheese melts.

To Freeze: Place in microwave-safe casserole; label and freeze for up to 2 months.

To Serve: Thaw. Cover with microwave-safe plastic wrap, and cook on High for 3 to 5 minutes.

Per Serving:		Diabetic Exchanges per Serving:	
calories:	299	milk:	0
protein (gm):	19.0	vegetable:	2
fat (gm):	8.5	fruit:	0
cholesterol (mg):	24	bread:	2
sodium (mg):	489	meat:	1
		fat:	1

Italian Vegetable Pita with Fresh Basil

2 medium tomatoes, seeded and diced
6 green onions, sliced thin
1 green pepper, diced
1 yellow squash, diced
2 small zucchini, diced
6 spinach leaves, chopped
1 cup basil leaves, chopped
2½ teaspoons tarragon vinegar
2 tablespoons olive oil
2 teaspoons Dijon mustard
1 teaspoon sugar
½ teaspoon black pepper, freshly ground
3 pita breads, cut in half

Serves 6.

Combine all ingredients except bread in a bowl. Toss to mix well. Drain off excess liquid, and spoon vegetables into each pita half.

To Freeze: Vacuum seal individual portions of filling; label and freeze for up to 2 months.

To Serve: Thaw in refrigerator, toss well, and spoon filling into pita halves.

Per Serving:		Diabetic Exchanges per Serving:	
calories:	172	milk:	0
protein (gm):	5.3	vegetable:	1
fat (gm):	5.3	fruit:	0
cholesterol (mg):	0	bread:	1½
sodium (mg):	222	meat:	0
		fat:	1

Midwestern Salmon Salad Pita

1 tablespoon Dijon-style mustard
½ teaspoon garlic powder
Freshly ground black pepper
1 tablespoon wine vinegar
¼ cup olive oil
¼ cup onion, chopped

4 ozs. spinach, torn into bite-size pieces and steamed until tender, about 8 minutes
4½ cups assorted lettuces, washed, dried, and torn into bite-size pieces
1 (15½-oz.) can salmon
2 whole-wheat pita breads, cut in half

Serves 4.

In a mixing bowl, combine mustard, garlic powder, pepper, and vinegar. Stir to mix, then slowly add olive oil, stirring constantly. Add onion. Whisk to blend. Toss the spinach and lettuces with the dressing. Add salmon and mix well. Spoon into pita halves.

To Freeze: Vacuum seal individual portions of filling; label and freeze for up to 2 months.

To Serve: Thaw in refrigerator, toss well, and spoon filling into pita halves.

Per Serving:		Diabetic Exchanges per Serving:	
calories:	395	milk:	0
protein (gm):	26.8	vegetable:	0
fat (gm):	21.3	fruit:	0
cholesterol (mg):	0	bread:	1½
sodium (mg):	736	meat:	3
		fat:	3

Tex Mex Pitas

½ cup plain low-fat yogurt
¼ cup Salsa (see Index)
1 lb. ground turkey
1 tablespoon garlic, minced

1 teaspoon pepper, cracked
1 tablespoon chili powder
1 cup onion, chopped
1 can zesty tomato soup
4 pita breads, cut in half
Shredded lettuce
1 cup tomato, diced
Serves 8.

Combine yogurt and Salsa and set aside. Cook turkey, garlic, pepper, chili powder, and onion in a pot until meat loses its pink color. Drain off spices. Return meat to pot and add tomato soup. Cook 15 minutes on medium heat. Adjust seasonings if needed. Spread some salsa mixture into each pita half, then spoon in turkey filling. Garnish with shredded lettuce and tomato.

To Freeze: Vacuum seal individual portions; label and freeze for up to 2 months.

To Serve: Put bags in boiling water, and bring to a boil again. Boil 10 to 12 minutes.

Per Serving:		Diabetic Exchanges per Serving:	
calories:	249	milk:	0
protein (gm):	17.4	vegetable:	1
fat (gm):	7.2	fruit:	0
cholesterol (mg):	38	bread:	1½
sodium (mg):	555	meat:	2
		fat:	0

1 package active dry yeast
1¼ to 1½ cups warm water,
   about 115°
⅛ teaspoon sugar
4 cups white flour
½ teaspoon salt
2 teaspoons vegetable oil
Serves 8.

The secret for success is in rolling the dough to the proper thickness, allowing it to rise to the proper thickness, and baking it in the center of a very hot oven on a heated, greased baking sheet.

Sprinkle yeast over ¼ cup of the warm water and stir until yeast is dissolved. Add sugar and set in a warm place until mixture begins to become foamy, about 5 minutes.

Meanwhile, sift flour and salt together into a bowl. Make a well in the center, and add yeast mixture. Mix well, adding enough of the warm water to make a slightly firm but not stiff dough.

Turn out onto floured board and knead about 15 minutes, working in the oil a teaspoon at a time, until dough is smooth and elastic. Place in oiled bowl; turn dough over to make sure it is oiled all over. Cover bowl with plastic wrap and set in a warm place to rise until double in bulk, about 2 hours.

Punch down dough and knead again on floured board for a few minutes. Divide dough into 6 or 8 equal parts. Flatten and shape each with the hands into patties. Dust each with flour, and roll out on floured board with floured rolling pin to exactly ¼-in. thickness. Measure with a ruler. (This is an important step and not as easy to judge as it may seem.)

Place a clean dish towel on a tray or board and sprinkle with flour. Lay rolled-out pitas on towel, leaving spaces in-between. You will need 2 or 3 trays for this operation. Cover pitas with another clean towel sprinkled with flour, the flour rubbed in.

Allow to rise in a warm place until exactly ½ in. high, again measuring with a ruler. This rising will take 30 to 45 minutes. Meanwhile, place oven rack in center of oven. You will be baking only one pan at a time unless you have a huge oven.

Preheat oven to 500°. A minute or two before ready to bake, place a greased baking sheet in the oven. When it is very hot, but not smoking, remove it and place 2 or 3 pitas on it. Bake about 6 minutes. Watch carefully so that pitas do not scorch.

Remove from baking sheet and cool on wire rack. With a brush (not a nylon brush, which will melt), regrease the baking sheet and continue baking the pitas. If not using the pitas immedi-

ately, or on the day of baking, wrap in plastic wrap before completely cooled and refrigerate or freeze. To serve, unwrap and heat
in oven until just heated through. It will only take a few minutes.

To Freeze: Vacuum seal individual pitas; label and freeze for up
to 2 months.

To Serve: Thaw on countertop and heat in microwave or oven if
desired.

Per Serving:		Diabetic Exchanges per Serving:	
calories:	222	milk:	0
protein (gm):	6.3	vegetable:	0
fat (gm):	1.6	fruit:	0
cholesterol (mg):	0	bread:	3
sodium (mg):	134	meat:	0
		fat:	0

Whole- Wheat Pita Bread

Prepare as for Pita Bread, above, with the following exceptions: Substitute 3 cups whole-wheat flour and 1 cup white flour for the 4 cups of white flour. Decrease the amount of vegetable oil to 1½ teaspoons.

The first rising will take less time than the white-flour pita; it can take as little as 1¼ hours. Reduce baking time by about 1 minute.

Serves 8.

To Freeze: Freeze as above.

To Serve: Thaw and reheat as above.

Per Serving:		Diabetic Exchanges per Serving:	
calories:	215	milk:	0
protein (gm):	8.0	vegetable:	0
fat (gm):	1.8	fruit:	0
cholesterol (mg):	0	bread:	3
sodium (mg):	136	meat:	0
		fat:	0

4

SIMMER-ON SOUPS

Beef Stock

½ cup dried mushrooms
2 lbs. short ribs of beef
2 lbs. beef marrow bones, cut into pieces
1 lb. ground beef chuck
1 large onion, peeled and coarsely chopped
1 clove garlic, peeled
4 medium carrots, cut into quarters
2 tablespoons Spike
10 peppercorns
1 bay leaf
1 teaspoon basil
1 teaspoon thyme
3 sprigs parsley
3 stalks celery
1 cup dry red wine
1 tablespoon soy sauce
Water

Makes about 3½ quarts.
Serves 20.

Soak the dried mushrooms in 1 cup of warm water for 15 minutes. Put all the ingredients, including the water in which the mushrooms were soaked, into a 6- or 8-qt. stockpot. Cover with cold water, 2 in. over ingredients. Place a loose-fitting lid on top and bring to a boil. Immediately, adjust heat to a simmer, and simmer for 3 to 4 hours. Turn off heat and cool.

When cool, strain all the stock into microwave-safe containers and refrigerate. When cold, remove and discard all the fat congealed on the surface. Refrigerate the stock for immediate use, or freeze for future use.

To Freeze: Place in microwave-safe casserole; label and freeze for up to 2 months.

To Serve: Thaw. Cover with microwave-safe plastic wrap, and cook on High for 3 to 5 minutes.

Per Serving:		Diabetic Exchanges per Serving:	
calories:	16	milk:	0
protein (gm):	2.7	vegetable:	0
fat (gm):	0.5	fruit:	0
cholesterol (mg):	0	bread:	0
sodium (mg):	42	meat:	0
		fat:	0

35

Chicken Stock

1 4-lb. chicken or 5-lb. fowl
2½ lbs. chicken necks and wings
1 veal knuckle, cracked (optional)
2 medium onions, stuck with several cloves
6 medium carrots, cut into quarters
2 medium leeks, cut into 1-in. pieces
3 stalks celery, including leaves
½ teaspoon basil
½ teaspoon thyme
½ teaspoon tarragon
1 garlic clove, peeled
2 tablespoons Spike
10 peppercorns
6 sprigs parsley
1 cup dry white wine
Cold water

Makes about 4 quarts.
Serves 16.

Place all the ingredients into a large 10-qt. stockpot. Add cold water to cover by 2 in. Place a loose-fitting lid on top and bring to a boil. Immediately adjust heat to a simmer, and simmer 3 to 4 hours. Turn off the heat and cool.

When cool, strain all the stock into microwave-safe containers and refrigerate. When cold, remove and discard all the fat congealed on the surface. Refrigerate the stock for immediate use, or freeze for future use.

To Freeze: Place in microwave-safe casserole; label and freeze for up to 2 months.

To Serve: Thaw. Cover with microwave-safe plastic wrap, and cook on High for 3 to 5 minutes.

Per Serving:		Diabetic Exchanges per Serving:	
calories:	39	milk:	0
protein (gm):	4.9	vegetable:	0
fat (gm):	1.3	fruit:	0
cholesterol (mg):	1	bread:	0
sodium (mg):	36	meat:	½
		fat:	0

Fish Stock

This stock is quick and easy to prepare. Keep a small batch on hand for soup, rice, or for a fish sauce. I like to freeze it in cup portions.

1½ lbs. fresh or frozen fish
1 medium onion, finely
   chopped
3 stalks celery with leaves, cut in half
1 medium carrot, finely diced
3 sprigs parsley
3 slices lemon
8 peppercorns
2 teaspoons Spike
¾ cup white wine
3 cups cold water

Makes about 3½ cups.
Serves 20.

Put all ingredients into a stockpot. Bring to a boil. Cover with a loose-fitting lid, and immediately adjust the heat to a simmer. Simmer for 30 minutes. Turn off heat and cool.

When cool, strain into a microwave-safe container. Refrigerate the stock if you are planning to use it within a day or two. Otherwise, store in freezer for future use.

To Freeze: Place in microwave-safe containers; label and freeze for up to 2 months.

To Serve: Thaw and use as desired, or microwave on High 3 to 4 minutes.

Per Serving:		Diabetic Exchanges per Serving:	
calories:	16	milk:	0
protein (gm):	2.7	vegetable:	0
fat (gm):	0.5	fruit:	0
cholesterol (mg):	0	bread:	0
sodium (mg):	42	meat:	0
		fat:	0

Carrot Soup with Dill

2 cups raw carrots, sliced
¼ cup green onions with tops, chopped
3 tablespoons fresh parsley, chopped

1 tablespoon diet margarine
1 tablespoon arrowroot
1½ cups Chicken Stock (see recipe p. 36)
½ cup evaporated skim milk
⅛ cup fresh dill, chopped
Serves 4.

Steam carrots about 20 minutes. Put aside. In stockpot cook on-ions and parsley in margarine until onions are softened. Sprinkle with arrowroot and cook, stirring occasionally, 2 minutes. Remove pot from heat and gradually blend in Chicken Stock. Return to heat; cook and stir until smooth and slightly thickened.

Place carrots in blender, and pour in 1 cup of stock mixture. Blend until smooth. Place carrot mixture in pot with stock and add skim milk. Heat gently (do not boil) and cook 2 minutes more. La-dle into soup cups and sprinkle with dill.

To Freeze: Place in microwave-safe casserole; label and freeze for up to 2 months.

To Serve: Thaw. Cover with microwave-safe plastic wrap, and cook on High for 3 to 5 minutes.

Per Serving:		Diabetic Exchanges per Serving:	
calories:	87	milk:	½
protein (gm):	5.0	vegetable:	1
fat (gm):	2.0	fruit:	0
cholesterol (mg):	2	bread:	0
sodium (mg):	382	meat:	0
		fat:	½

Egg Drop Soup

2 scallions
2 egg whites

2 tablespoons cornstarch
2 tablespoons water
6 cups Chicken Stock (see
   page 36)
White pepper to taste
Serves 8.

Wash and cut scallions into 1-in. pieces. Set aside. Beat egg whites thoroughly. Set aside.

Dissolve 1 tablespoon cornstarch in 2 tablespoons cold water. Heat Chicken Stock in saucepan until it boils. Add cornstarch slowly until stock thickens gradually. Add scallions and stir a few times. Remove from heat. Stir in egg whites with a fork. Serve, letting each person add pepper to taste.

To Freeze: Place in microwave-safe casserole; label and freeze for up to 2 months.

To Serve: Thaw. Cover with microwave-safe plastic wrap, and cook on High for 3 to 5 minutes.

Per Serving:		Diabetic Exchanges per Serving:	
calories:	41	milk:	0
protein (gm):	4.6	vegetable:	0
fat (gm):	1.0	fruit:	0
cholesterol (mg):	0	bread:	0
sodium (mg):	48	meat:	1
		fat:	0

Gazpacho

3 cups tomatoes, peeled, seeded, and chopped

1½ cups no-salt-added tomato juice

¾ cup cucumber, peeled, seeded, and chopped

⅓ cup onion, chopped

⅓ cup green bell pepper, chopped

2 tablespoons balsamic vinegar

¼ teaspoon hot sauce

1 clove garlic, minced

4 cucumber slices and 4 teaspoons minced green bell pepper (for garnish)

Makes 5 cups.

Serves 4.

Combine first 5 ingredients in container of blender; top with cover and process until almost smooth. Pour into large bowl. Stir in vinegar and next two ingredients; cover and chill at least 2 hours. Garnish with cucumber slices and minced bell pepper, if desired. Serve chilled.

To Freeze: Place in microwave-safe casserole; label and freeze for up to 2 months.

To Serve: Thaw. Cover with microwave-safe plastic wrap, and cook on High for 3 to 5 minutes. Garnish with cucumber slices and minced bell pepper.

Per Serving:		Diabetic Exchanges per Serving:	
calories:	71	milk:	0
protein (gm):	3.0	vegetable:	3
fat (gm):	0.6	fruit:	0
cholesterol (mg):	0	bread:	0
sodium (mg):	29	meat:	0
		fat:	0

Mushroom Barley Soup with Herbs

2 tablespoons vegetable oil
2 cups onions, finely chopped
1 cup carrots, diced
½ cup celery, finely chopped
1 lb. mushrooms, sliced
1 teaspoon garlic, minced
½ teaspoon celery seed
1 teaspoon thyme

1 teaspoon basil
1 teaspoon tarragon
2 cups Beef Stock (see page 35)
2 cups Chicken Stock (see page 36)
2 cups water
½ cup pearl barley
3 tablespoons fresh parsley, chopped

Serves 8.

Heat oil in stockpot and add onions, carrots, and celery. Cover and cook, stirring occasionally, until tender, about 5 minutes. Stir in mushrooms, garlic, and herbs; cook covered 3 minutes more. Add Beef Stock, Chicken Stock, and 2 cups water to pot. Add barley. Bring to boil, reduce heat, and simmer covered 1½ hours. Freeze or sprinkle parsley on soup and serve.

To Freeze: Place in microwave-safe casserole; label and freeze for up to 2 months.

To Serve: Thaw. Cover with microwave-safe plastic wrap, and cook on High for 3 to 5 minutes.

Per Serving:		Diabetic Exchanges per Serving:	
calories:	124	milk:	0
protein (gm):	5.0	vegetable:	1½
fat (gm):	4.4	fruit:	0
cholesterol (mg):	0	bread:	1
sodium (mg):	405	meat:	0
		fat:	½

Mushroom Soup Danielle

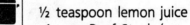

This is a soup with real flavor. It is very simple to prepare and can be frozen.

1 lb. fresh or frozen
   mushrooms
4 tablespoons diet unsalted
   margarine
½ teaspoon lemon juice
4 cups Beef Stock (see
   page 35)
4 teaspoons low-sodium soy
   sauce
1½ tablespoons potato flour
3 tablespoons cold water
2 tablespoons sherry
3 tablespoons chives,
   chopped

Serves 6.

Clean mushrooms. Set aside 4 mushroom caps. Coarsely chop remainder of mushrooms, including stems.

Melt margarine in a large pot, and add mushrooms and lemon juice. Cook over medium-high heat 3 or 4 minutes, stirring constantly. Add beef stock and soy sauce. Cover pot and simmer 5 minutes.

Pour mixture into a blender or food processor and blend until smooth. Pour back into pot, and bring to simmer. Mix potato flour with cold water and stir into soup. Continue to cook until thickened.

Slice raw mushroom caps and add to soup. Continue to simmer 5 minutes. Remove from heat, and add sherry before serving topped with chives.

To Freeze: Place in microwave-safe casserole; label and freeze for up to 2 months.

To Serve: Thaw. Cover with microwave-safe plastic wrap, and cook on High for 3 to 5 minutes.

Per Serving:		Diabetic Exchanges per Serving:	
calories:	83	milk:	0
protein (gm):	4.0	vegetable:	1
fat (gm):	4.5	fruit:	0
cholesterol (mg):	0	bread:	0
sodium (mg):	61	meat:	0
		fat:	1

Onion Soup

This soup is best if you allow the stock to simmer slowly so that the stock and onions meld their flavors. Don't be in a rush to tenderize the onions by trying to boil it up fast.

2 tablespoons diet no-salt-added margarine
2 tablespoons olive oil

4 cups onions, peeled and sliced into thin rings
2 tablespoons flour
¼ teaspoon pepper
8 cups hot Beef Stock (see page 35)
¼ cup brandy
8 thick slices French bread, toasted
1 cup Parmesan cheese, grated

Serves 8.

Melt margarine and oil in large heavy pot and add onions. Keep heat low and cook and stir slowly until onions are golden. Sprinkle flour on and mix well. Add pepper.

Remove from heat and slowly add beef stock, stirring continuously. When well blended, return to heat and bring to boil. Adjust heat to simmer, cover pot, and simmer 35 to 45 minutes. Add brandy.

To serve: Ladle soup into deep, oven-safe soup bowls, place a piece of toasted French bread on top of each bowl of soup, and heap a generous tablespoon of cheese of top of bread. Place under broiler until cheese has melted and is lightly browned. Serve immediately or freeze.

To Freeze: Place in microwave-safe casserole; label and freeze for up to 2 months.

To Serve: Thaw. Cover with microwave-safe plastic wrap, and cook on High for 3 to 5 minutes.

Per Serving:		Diabetic Exchanges per Serving:	
calories:	265	milk:	0
protein (gm):	12.4	vegetable:	1
fat (gm):	10.7	fruit:	0
cholesterol (mg):	10	bread:	1½
sodium (mg):	750	meat:	1
		fat:	1½

Pasta Fagioli

1 cup dried pinto beans
3 cups Chicken Stock (see page 36)
1¼ cups onion, chopped
½ cup celery, chopped
1¼ cups carrots, sliced
2½ cups tomatoes, diced

1 cup green bell pepper, diced
1 clove garlic, minced
1 teaspoon oregano
1 teaspoon basil
½ teaspoon rosemary
¼ teaspoon red (cayenne) pepper, ground
½ cup cooked macaroni
Serves 8.

Put beans in stockpot and cover with water. Cook, covered, till almost tender, a little over 1 hour. Drain; return to stockpot.

Add Chicken Stock and onion and cook, covered, 20 minutes. Add remaining vegetables and seasonings. Cook, covered, 20 to 30 minutes or longer. Add macaroni and more broth if necessary; heat through and serve or freeze.

To Freeze: Place in microwave-safe casserole; label and freeze for up to 2 months.

To Serve: Thaw. Cover with microwave-safe plastic wrap, and cook on High for 3 to 5 minutes.

Per Serving:		Diabetic Exchanges per Serving:	
calories:	114	milk:	0
protein (gm):	6.6	vegetable:	1
fat (gm):	0.9	fruit:	0
cholesterol (mg):	0	bread:	1
sodium (mg):	190	meat:	0
		fat:	0

5

THE ACTIVE POTATO

AND

OTHER VEGGIES

To Roast Peppers

Place fresh peppers directly over a gas flame or under the broiler as close to the heat as possible, turning frequently until charred all over. Enclose the peppers in a paper or plastic bag and set aside for 10 minutes to steam. When cool enough to handle, peel off the skins. Rinse to remove any charred bits. Using a small sharp knife, remove the core, seeds, and ribs.

To Sun-Dry Tomatoes

Use Italian tomatoes, plum or Roma. Cover an oven rack or cake rack with cheesecloth. Cut tomatoes in half lengthwise and place them, cut side up, on the cheesecloth. Cover with another piece of cheesecloth. Take tomatoes outside and keep in full sun 2 to 3 days. Be sure to bring them in at night, or you may find them gone in the morning (critters, you know). They're perfect when dry and shriveled but flexible, not brittle. Pack loosely in jars and pour virgin olive oil to cover. You may also add fresh basil leaves, parsley or rosemary if you like. Cover tightly and keep in pantry. I have kept sun-dried tomatoes more than a year, and the oil still tasted fine.

Marinated Broccoli

3 bunches broccoli, without stems
1¼ cups safflower oil
1 cup balsamic vinegar
1 tablespoon dill weed

1 tablespoon red wine vinegar
2 tablespoons red wine
1 teaspoon garlic salt
1 teaspoon Spike
1 tablespoon soy sauce
Fresh dill or nasturtium blossoms for garnish

Serves 6.

Separate broccoli into florets. Combine remaining ingredients in blender. Blend till mixed well. Pour over broccoli and marinate 4 to 24 hours. Before serving, pour off marinade and garnish with dill or nasturtiums.

To Freeze: Vacuum seal broccoli with marinade; label and freeze for up to 2 months.

To Serve: Defrost, pour off marinade, and garnish with dill.

Per Serving:		Diabetic Exchanges per Serving:	
calories:	52	milk:	0
protein (gm):	1.3	vegetable:	1
fat (gm):	4.6	fruit:	0
cholesterol (mg):	0	bread:	0
sodium (mg):	29	meat:	0
		fat:	½

Creamed Onions and Mushrooms

This is a classic Thanksgiving treat that is good anytime.

4 tablespoons diet margarine

2 tablespoons arrowroot
1¾ cups skim milk
1 teaspoon Spike
2 lbs. small white onions (12 per lb.), peeled
1 cup mushrooms, sliced
Freshly ground black pepper

Serves 8.

Heat 2 tablespoons of the margarine in a 10-in. casserole, un-covered, and cook on High for 1 minute. Whisk in arrowroot and cook uncovered on High for 2 minutes more.

Remove from microwave oven. Whisk in milk and Spike, stir-ring well. Add onions and stir to coat. Cover tightly with plastic wrap. Cook on High 10 minutes.

Remove from microwave. Uncover and stir in remaining mar-garine and pepper.

To Freeze: Vacuum seal individual portions; label and freeze for up to 2 months.

To Serve: Put bags in boiling water, and bring to a boil again. Boil 10 to 12 minutes.

Per Serving:		Diabetic Exchanges per Serving:	
calories:	91	milk:	0
protein (gm):	3.3	vegetable:	2
fat (gm):	3.2	fruit:	0
cholesterol (mg):	0	bread:	0
sodium (mg):	95	meat:	0
		fat:	½

Steamed Carrots and Pea Pods

6 medium carrots (3 cups), sliced

6 to 8 ozs. pea pods
Pepper, freshly ground
3 tablespoons diet unsalted margarine
Serves 6.

Pour boiling water into wok to reach about ½ in. below steamer rack. Arrange carrots on steamer rack in wok. Cover and steam 15 minutes. Add pea pods and steam an additional 3 to 5 minutes. Remove vegetables to serving plate, and season with freshly ground pepper and margarine.

To Freeze: Vacuum seal individual portions; label and freeze for up to 2 months.

To Serve: Put bags in boiling water, and bring to a boil again. Boil 10 to 12 minutes.

Per Serving:		Diabetic Exchanges per Serving:	
calories:	86	milk:	0
protein (gm):	2.7	vegetable:	2
fat (gm):	3.1	fruit:	0
cholesterol (mg):	0	bread:	0
sodium (mg):	28	meat:	0
		fat:	½

Green and Gold Stir-Fry

2 tablespoons vegetable oil
1 cup leeks, thinly sliced
1 cup green bell pepper, chopped
1 cup yellow bell pepper, chopped

2 cups broccoli florets
2 cups yellow summer squash, cut in wedges
1 tablespoon dried garlic, minced
1 tablespoon oregano
2 tablespoons basil
2 tablespoons fresh chives, minced
Serves 6.

Heat wok and add vegetable oil and leeks. Stir-fry 2 minutes. Add green and yellow peppers, and stir-fry 1 more minute. Add broccoli and yellow squash with dried garlic, and stir-fry about 3 minutes or until crisp-tender. Add herbs and chives, and stir-fry 1 more minute.

To Freeze: Vacuum seal individual portions; label and freeze for up to 2 months.

To Reheat: Put bags in boiling water, and bring to a boil again. Boil 10 to 12 minutes.

Per Serving:		Diabetic Exchanges per Serving:	
calories:	79	milk:	0
protein (gm):	1.9	vegetable:	1½
fat (gm):	5.0	fruit:	0
cholesterol (mg):	0	bread:	0
sodium (mg):	13	meat:	0
		fat:	1

...ed
... Pepper
Stir-Fry

Vegetable cooking spray
3 tablespoons white wine
1 green pepper, cut into
   julienne strips
1 red pepper, cut into julienne
   strips

1 yellow pepper, cut into
   julienne strips
1 medium onion, sliced
¼ cup green onions, sliced
1 tablespoon fresh basil,
   minced
¼ teaspoon fresh thyme
1 teaspoon garlic powder
2 tablespoons fresh parsley

Serves 4.

Coat a wok with cooking spray; place over high heat until hot.
Add wine, peppers, onion slices, green onions, basil, thyme, and
garlic powder. Stir-fry 3 to 3½ minutes or until vegetables are
crisp-tender. If serving as a vegetable, place peppers in a bowl and
garnish with parsley.

To Freeze: Vacuum seal, label, and freeze for up to 2 months.

To Serve: Place bags in boiling water, and bring water to a boil
again. Boil 10 to 12 minutes.

Per Serving:		Diabetic Exchanges per Serving:	
calories:	35	milk:	0
protein (gm):	1.0	vegetable:	1
fat (gm):	0.3	fruit:	0
cholesterol (mg):	0	bread:	0
sodium (mg):	9	meat:	0
		fat:	0

Acorn Squash with Cranberry Topping

This dish is colorful and contains no fat, making it ideal for company.

1 large acorn squash (about 2 lbs.)

½ cup cranberries
3 tablespoons orange juice concentrate, divided
1 tablespoon water
1 tablespoon dark raisins
4 packets Equal® or 4 teaspoons sugar

Serves 4.

Cut squash in half and place, cut side down, in glass pie plate; add 1 tablespoon water. Cover loosely with wax paper. Microwave on High 8 to 10 minutes, until tender, rotating plate a half-turn halfway through. Set aside.

Combine cranberries, 2 tablespoons orange juice concentrate, 1 tablespoon water, raisins, and sugar in 4-cup glass measure. Microwave 4 to 5 minutes, stirring once halfway through, until slightly thickened.

Drain squash and cut each half lengthwise in half. Return each quarter, cut side up, to pie plate; brush with remaining 1 tablespoon orange juice concentrate. Top evenly with cranberry mixture. Microwave 30 seconds to 1 minute.

To Freeze: Place in microwave-safe casserole; label and freeze for up to 2 months.

To Serve: Thaw. Cover with microwave-safe plastic wrap, and cook on High for 3 to 5 minutes.

Per Serving:		Diabetic Exchanges per Serving:	
calories:	157	milk:	0
protein (gm):	2.8	vegetable:	0
fat (gm):	0.4	fruit:	2
cholesterol (mg):	0	bread:	1½
sodium (mg):	10	meat:	0
		fat:	0

Fruit-Filled Squash

2 small acorn squash (about 1 lb. each)
1 small baking apple, cored and thinly sliced

1 medium-size Bartlett pear, cored and thinly sliced
½ cup packed brown sugar
Ground cinnamon or allspice
Lemon juice
¼ cup raisins
½ cup Butter Buds
¼ cup water
Serves 4.

Cut squash in half lengthwise; remove seeds. Arrange one-fourth of fruit on top of each squash half. Sprinkle each half with 2 tablespoons brown sugar, dash of cinnamon or allspice, and a few drops of lemon juice. Top each half with 1 tablespoon raisins and 1 tablespoon Butter Buds. Wrap each squash half in foil.

Pour ¼ cup water into crockpot. Stack squash, cut side up, in pot and cover. Cook on Low heat 5½ to 6 hours or on High 4 to 4½ hours.

Lift squash halves from pot; remove foil. Drain any syrup in foil into saucepan and serve with squash.

Note: Other fruits such as oranges, peaches, nectarines, or pineapple may be substituted for the apples and pears.

To Freeze: Place in microwave-safe casserole; label and freeze for up to 2 months.

To Serve: Thaw. Cover with microwave-safe plastic wrap, and cook on High for 3 to 5 minutes.

Per Serving:		Diabetic Exchanges per Serving:	
calories:	272	milk:	0
protein (gm):	2.1	vegetable:	0
fat (gm):	3.2	fruit:	1
cholesterol (mg):	0	bread:	3
sodium (mg):	322	meat:	0
		fat:	0

Ali Baba Casserole

4 medium-size sweet potatoes, peeled and cut into ½-in. dice (about 4 cups)
2 large onions, cut into ½-in. dice (about 2 cups)
3 cups cooked garbanzo beans (may be canned)
1 cup Chicken Stock (see page 36)
½ cup red bell pepper, diced
½ cup mushrooms, sliced

3 cups zucchini, sliced
1 cup yellow squash, sliced
2 large, fresh, ripe tomatoes, seeded and cut into ½-in. dice

Sauce:
1 tablespoon lemon juice
½ teaspoon red (cayenne) pepper, ground
½ teaspoon garlic powder
¼ teaspoon saffron
½ teaspoon coriander, ground
¾ teaspoon cinnamon, ground
Serves 8.

Combine sweet potatoes, onions, garbanzos, and Chicken Stock in large stockpot. Bring to boil, reduce heat, and simmer, covered, 20 minutes or until onions and potatoes are almost tender. Add remaining vegetables and cook, covered, 10 minutes. Uncover and cook 10 minutes longer.

Combine sauce ingredients in small saucepan and heat till spices dissolve. Mixture will resemble paste. Add to cooked vegetables; cook, uncovered, 5 minutes. Serve over brown rice or freeze.

To Freeze: Place in microwave-safe casserole; label and freeze for up to 2 months.

To Serve: Thaw. Cover with microwave-safe plastic wrap, and cook on High for 3 to 5 minutes.

Per Serving:		Diabetic Exchanges per Serving:	
calories:	233	milk:	0
protein (gm):	10.9	vegetable:	1
fat (gm):	2.3	fruit:	0
cholesterol (mg):	0	bread:	2
sodium (mg):	118	meat:	1
		fat:	0

Eggplant Parmesan

1 medium eggplant
1 6-oz. can low-sodium tomato
   paste
1 cup water
1 (14½-oz.) can low-sodium
   chunky tomatoes

1 tablespoon oregano
1 tablespoon basil
1 cup mozzarella cheese,
   shredded
3 tablespoons Parmesan cheese,
   grated
Serves 4.

Pare eggplant; cut into ⅛-in. thick slices.

In a bowl, combine tomato paste, water, and tomatoes. Mix well. Add oregano and basil. Spread sauce on bottom of 2-qt. casserole. Layer half of eggplant, more sauce, and half the mozzarella cheese. Repeat layers. Finish by sprinkling Parmesan cheese on top. Cover casserole.

Place in microwave and cook on High 14 to 16 minutes, giving dish a quarter-turn after 8 minutes. Continue to cook 1 to 2 minutes until all cheese has melted.

To Freeze: Label casserole and freeze for up to 2 months.

To Serve: Thaw and place in microwave on High for 7 to 9 minutes.

Per Serving:		Diabetic Exchanges per Serving:	
calories:	230	milk:	0
protein (gm):	18.6	vegetable:	3
fat (gm):	11.2	fruit:	0
cholesterol (mg):	36	bread:	0
sodium (mg):	349	meat:	2
		fat:	1

Moo Shu Vegetables

2 tablespoons peanut oil
2 large garlic cloves, minced
12 large green onions, sliced
1 thin slice fresh ginger, the size of a quarter, minced
½ red bell pepper, chopped
½ medium head Chinese cabbage, thinly sliced
1 medium carrot, shredded
12 small mushrooms, sliced
2 small zucchini, diced
1 tablespoon soy sauce
1 tablespoon rice vinegar (sushi vinegar)
1½ tablespoons Hoisin sauce
1 teaspoon sugar
1 teaspoon oriental sesame oil
2 tablespoons dry sherry mixed with 1 teaspoon cornstarch
8 Mandarin pancakes, steamed (see Note)
Hoisin sauce, for serving
Serves 4.

Add oil to hot wok, then add garlic, green onions, ginger, red bell pepper, cabbage, carrot, mushrooms, and zucchini. Stir-fry over high heat until vegetables are hot, about 3 minutes. Add soy sauce, vinegar, Hoisin, sugar, sesame oil, and sherry mixture. Cook until thickened, about 3 minutes, stirring often. Can be made in advance and reheated stove-top.

To serve, place scant ½ cup hot vegetable mixture in middle of each pancake. Bring two sides of pancake up to close, then bring ends over to seal package. Serve seam side up with Hoisin sauce.

Note: To steam pancakes on stove top, place over boiling water in flat-bottomed steamer. Cover and steam over moderate heat until pancakes are hot and soft, about 5 minutes. To steam in microwave oven, wrap pancakes in damp paper towels, place on microwave dish, and heat at Medium (50 percent) until warm, about 2 to 3 minutes, turning over midway. Wrap steamed pancakes in cloth towel to keep warm and soft until filled.

To Freeze: Vacuum seal individual vegetable portions; label and freeze for up to 2 months.

To Serve: Put bags in boiling water, and bring water to a boil again. Boil 10 to 12 minutes.

Per Serving:		Diabetic Exchanges per Serving:	
calories:	439	milk:	0
protein (gm):	8.6	vegetable:	1
fat (gm):	17.7	fruit:	0
cholesterol (mg):	0	bread:	3
sodium (mg):	328	meat:	0
		fat:	4

Stuffed Cabbage Rolls with Tomato Sauce

1 medium green cabbage
1 lb. mushrooms, chopped
¼ cup raw converted rice
1 cup drained canned
    tomatoes
2 egg whites, slightly beaten
1 medium onion, peeled and
    grated
1 medium carrot, peeled and
    grated
1 teaspoon Spike
¼ cup vinegar
½ cup light-brown sugar, firmly
    packed
1 cup canned tomato sauce
Serves 5.

Drop cabbage into stockpot of boiling water and cook 4 to 8 minutes or until outer leaves come off easily. Drain and cool. Remove 10 of the large outer leaves and set aside. Discard tough inner core and chop up rest of cabbage. Spread chopped cabbage over bottom of crockpot.

In a bowl, combine mushrooms, rice, and tomatoes. Add egg whites and mix well. Add onion, carrot, and Spike and mix again. Spread some of mixture in center of each large cabbage leaf, leaving a flap on either side. Roll up leaves and tuck in side flaps. Place rolls in crockpot.

In a small bowl, combine vinegar, sugar, and tomato sauce and pour over rolls. Cover crockpot and cook on Low 8 to 10 hours.

To Freeze: Place in microwave-safe casserole; label and freeze for up to 2 months.

To Serve: Thaw in refrigerator and place in microwave. Microwave on High 7 to 9 minutes. Garnish before serving.

Per Serving:		Diabetic Exchanges per Serving:	
calories:	195	milk:	0
protein (gm):	6.0	vegetable:	2
fat (gm):	0.8	fruit:	0
cholesterol (mg):	0	bread:	2
sodium (mg):	421	meat:	0
		fat:	0

Avocado-Topped Potatoes

4 large baking potatoes
Vegetable oil
1 8-oz. container plain low-fat
  yogurt

1 ripe avocado, pee
  mashed
2 tablespoons skim ....
1 tablespoon lemon juice
1 tablespoon onion, grated
¼ teaspoon Spike
¼ cup imitation bacon bits
2 tomatoes, cut into wedges
Serves 8.

Rub potatoes with oil. Bake in microwave oven on High for 9 minutes.

Meanwhile, prepare avocado topping. Mix well all ingredients except bacon bits and tomatoes in a bowl. Split tops of potatoes lengthwise, and fluff pulp with a fork. Spoon avocado topping over potatoes. Sprinkle with bacon bits and garnish with tomato wedges.

To Freeze: Prepare avocado topping and place in vacuum-sealed bags; label and freeze for up to 2 months.

To Serve: Thaw avocado topping in refrigerator, bake potatoes, fill with topping, and garnish with bacon bits and tomato wedges.

Per Serving:		Diabetic Exchanges per Serving:	
calories:	169	milk:	0
protein (gm):	4.8	vegetable:	0
fat (gm):	7.3	fruit:	0
cholesterol (mg):	1	bread:	1
sodium (mg):	113	meat:	0
		fat:	2

Broccoli-Chicken Topped Potatoes

4 medium potatoes
Vegetable oil
1 package (10 ozs.) broccoli, chopped, thawed, and drained

1 teaspoon basil
1 teaspoon oregano
1½ cups cooked or canned chicken
1 (10-oz.) jar pimiento, drained
¼ cup green onions, sliced
4 tablespoons Parmesan cheese, grated

Serves 8.

Coat potatoes with vegetable oil and bake in microwave on High about 10 minutes. Place broccoli, basil, oregano, chicken, pimiento, and green onions in microwave bowl. Microwave on High 5 minutes or until mixture is hot.

Split tops of potatoes lengthwise, and fluff pulp with a fork. Spoon topping over potatoes. Top with Parmesan cheese.

To Freeze: Place in microwave-safe containers; label and freeze for up to 2 months.

To Serve: Thaw and microwave on High 7 to 9 minutes.

Per Serving:		**Diabetic Exchanges per Serving:**	
calories:	134	milk:	0
protein (gm):	10.6	vegetable:	½
fat (gm):	1.8	fruit:	0
cholesterol (mg):	20	bread:	1
sodium (mg):	86	meat:	1
		fat:	0

Crabmeat-Topped Potatoes

4 large baking potatoes
Vegetable oil
1 tablespoon diet margarine
¼ cup green onions
¼ cup green bell pepper, chopped

1½ cups plain low-fat yogurt
1 can (6 ozs.) crabmeat,*
   drained and flaked
¼ cup skim milk
½ teaspoon white pepper
¼ teaspoon garlic powder
2 tablespoons chives, chopped

Serves 8.

Coat potatoes with vegetable oil and bake in microwave oven on High about 9 minutes.

Put margarine, onion, and green bell pepper in microwave dish and cook on High about 2 minutes. Add yogurt, crabmeat, and milk and cook on High 2 minutes more. Remove from microwave and stir in pepper and garlic powder.

Split tops of potatoes lengthwise, and fluff pulp with fork. Spoon topping over potatoes. Garnish with chives.

Shrimp may be used in place of crabmeat.

To Freeze: Place in microwave-safe containers; label and freeze for up to 2 months.

To Serve: Place in microwave on High 7 to 9 minutes.

Per Serving:		Diabetic Exchanges per Serving:	
calories:	151	milk:	0
protein (gm):	7.8	vegetable:	0
fat (gm):	4.2	fruit:	0
cholesterol (mg):	24	bread:	1
sodium (mg):	160	meat:	1
		fat:	½

Chili-Topped Potatoes

4 large baking potatoes
Vegetable oil
½ lb. ground turkey
⅓ cup onion, finely chopped
1 clove garlic, minced

1 cup canned tomato sauce
½ cup water
1 to 1½ tablespoons chili powder
¼ teaspoon Spike
½ cup low-cholesterol Cheddar cheese, shredded
Green onions, chopped
2 fresh tomatoes, quartered
Serves 8.

Rub potatoes with oil and bake in microwave oven on High 10 minutes.

Place turkey, onion, and garlic in microwave dish and cook on High 7 minutes. Add tomato sauce, water, chili powder, and Spike and continue cooking 5 to 6 minutes more. Remove from microwave and drain well.

Split tops of potatoes lengthwise, and fluff pulp with fork. Spoon topping over potatoes. Sprinkle with cheese and green onions and serve with tomatoes.

To Freeze: Place in microwave-safe container; label and freeze for up to 2 months.

To Serve: Place in microwave on High 7 to 9 minutes.

Per Serving:		Diabetic Exchanges per Serving:	
calories:	190	milk:	0
protein (gm):	13.6	vegetable:	1
fat (gm):	6.0	fruit:	0
cholesterol (mg):	24	bread:	1
sodium (mg):	421	meat:	1½
		fat:	½

Garden-Topped Potatoes

4 large baking potatoes
Vegetable oil
3 tablespoons diet margarine
1 large green bell pepper,
 chopped
1 cup green onions, sliced
1 clove garlic, crushed

½ cup mushrooms, sliced
1 cup zucchini, sliced
2 tomatoes, unpeeled and
 chopped
¾ cup evaporated skim milk
¼ cup Parmesan cheese, grated
¼ teaspoon Spike
Dash pepper
2 tablespoons fresh parsley,
 chopped

Serves 8.

Rub potatoes with oil and bake in microwave oven on High 10 minutes.

Melt margarine in stockpot; add green bell pepper, onions, and garlic and saute 2 to 3 minutes. Stir in mushrooms and zucchini and saute 1 to 2 minutes. Add tomatoes and cook 2 minutes. Stir in next four ingredients and cook until thoroughly heated.

Split tops of potatoes lengthwise, and fluff pulp with fork. Spoon topping over potatoes and garnish with parsley.

To Freeze: Place individual portions of topping in microwave-safe casserole; label and freeze for up to 2 months.

To Serve: Thaw, cover with microwave-safe plastic wrap, and microwave on High 4 to 7 minutes. Garnish if desired.

Per Serving:		Diabetic Exchanges per Serving:	
calories:	159	milk:	0
protein (gm):	5.4	vegetable:	1
fat (gm):	5.6	fruit:	0
cholesterol (mg):	3	bread:	1
sodium (mg):	142	meat:	0
		fat:	1

...an-
,opped
Potatoes

6 large baking potatoes
Vegetable oil
½ lb. bulk turkey sausage
1 lb. part-skim mozzarella
  cheese, cubed

¼ cup skim milk
2 cups Salsa (see Index) or 1
  can (10 ozs.) tomatoes and
  green chilies, undrained and
  chopped
Shredded lettuce
Chopped tomato
Serves 12.

Rub potatoes with oil and bake in microwave oven on High 10 minutes.

Cook sausage in microwave oven about 8 minutes on High. Drain and set aside.

Place cheese and milk in microwave dish and cook on High about 2 minutes or until cheese melts. Add to meat mixture, with Salsa, and mix well.

Split tops of potatoes lengthwise, and fluff pulp with fork. Spoon topping over potatoes. Sprinkle with lettuce and tomato.

To Freeze: Place in microwave-safe containers; label and freeze for up to 2 months.

To Serve: Place in microwave on High 7 to 9 minutes.

Per Serving:		Diabetic Exchanges per Serving:	
calories:	249	milk:	0
protein (gm):	16.6	vegetable:	1
fat (gm):	10.9	fruit:	0
cholesterol (mg):	37	bread:	1
sodium (mg):	398	meat:	2
		fat:	1

Greek Stuffed Zucchini

This is a very versatile dish because you can serve it for lunch or a light dinner. Just add a green salad and French bread.

10 6-in. zucchinis
½ cup cooked long grain rice
1½ cups onion, finely chopped
2 cups celery, finely chopped
1 teaspoon Spike
Pepper, freshly ground
1 teaspoon basil
1 teaspoon oregano
3 tablespoons olive oil
1 cup parsley, chopped
1 cup tomato, chopped
3 tablespoons lemon juice

Serves 6.

Slice zucchini in half lengthwise, and scoop out insides to make boats; set aside. In a bowl, add rice and remaining ingredients. Stuff mixture into zucchini boats. Place boats in microwave dish and microwave on High 10 minutes.

To Freeze: Place in microwave-safe casserole; label and freeze for up to 2 months.

To Serve: Thaw. Cover with microwave-safe plastic wrap, and cook on High for 3 to 5 minutes.

Per Serving:		Diabetic Exchanges per Serving:	
calories:	117	milk:	0
protein (gm):	2.1	vegetable:	1
fat (gm):	7.0	fruit:	0
cholesterol (mg):	0	bread:	½
sodium (mg):	13	meat:	0
		fat:	1

Gratin of Zucchini with Tomato

2 large zucchinis
1 can (14½ ozs.) chunky
   tomatoes

½ cup fresh basil, chopped
¼ cup fresh parsley, chopped
2 tablespoons cilantro
½ cup seasoned breadcrumbs
¼ cup Parmesan cheese, grated
1 tablespoon diet margarine
Serves 4.

Wash and trim zucchini. Cut lengthwise into ¼-in. slices. Dry zucchini with paper towels. Preheat oven to 375°.

In saucepan, heat chunky tomatoes, then add basil, parsley, and cilantro and simmer 3 minutes. Pour half of the tomato mixture into a shallow, 8×12-in. baking dish. Arrange zucchini slices on top, and cover with remaining tomato mixture. Combine breadcrumbs and Parmesan cheese and sprinkle over casserole. Dot with margarine.

Bake in 375° oven 30 to 40 minutes until zucchini is tender and crust golden. Serve piping hot or freeze.

To Freeze: Place in microwave-safe casserole; label and freeze for up to 2 months.

To Serve: Thaw. Cover with microwave-safe plastic wrap, and cook on High for 3 to 5 minutes.

Per Serving:		Diabetic Exchanges per Serving:	
calories:	123	milk:	0
protein (gm):	6.1	vegetable:	2
fat (gm):	4.3	fruit:	0
cholesterol (mg):	4	bread:	½
sodium (mg):	414	meat:	0
		fat:	1

Eggplant Lasagna

1 eggplant (1 lb.)
2 tablespoons water
Vegetable cooking spray
2 cans (8 ozs. each) tomato
  sauce

2 tablespoons olive oil
1 cup low-fat cottage cheese
Pepper, freshly ground
½ cup part-skim mozzarella
  cheese, shredded
4 tablespoons Parmesan cheese
Serves 4.

Peel and dice eggplant in ½-in. cubes. Put into 2-qt. casserole with 2 tablespoons water. Cover. Microwave on High 5 to 6 minutes, stirring halfway through cooking. Remove and drain.

Coat insides of four 1½- to 2-cup casseroles with vegetable cooking spray. Divide ½ cup tomato sauce evenly among casseroles. Divide half of eggplant evenly among casseroles. Divide olive oil among casseroles. Add pepper to cottage cheese and add to casseroles. Sprinkle with half of mozzarella. Divide 1 cup tomato sauce evenly among casseroles. Place remaining eggplant on top. Cover with remaining tomato sauce, mozzarella, and Parmesan.

Bake in preheated oven at 425° 20 to 25 minutes or until lightly browned and eggplant is cooked through.

Note: Instead of individual casseroles, lasagna may be made and baked in 8-in.-square baking dish. Increase baking time to 30 minutes.

To Freeze: Place individual portions in separate vacuum-sealed bags; label and freeze for up to 2 months.

To Serve: Put bags in boiling water, and bring water to a boil again. Boil 10 to 12 minutes. Add garnishes such as parsley or cheese just before serving.

Per Serving:		Diabetic Exchanges per Serving:	
calories:	252	milk:	0
protein (gm):	16.8	vegetable:	2
fat (gm):	12.2	fruit:	0
cholesterol (mg):	17	bread:	0
sodium (mg):	449	meat:	2
		fat:	2

6

THE SKINNY ON PASTA

Fettuccine with Asparagus and Shrimp in Parmesan Sauce

1 tablespoon plus 1 teaspoon diet margarine
1 cup sliced mushrooms
2 garlic cloves, minced
1 cup diagonally sliced steamed asparagus spears
1 egg white
¼ cup low-fat yogurt
½ cup skim milk
4 ozs. (½ cup) grated Parmesan cheese
Dash pepper, freshly ground
18 large shrimp, cooked or canned
1 lb. fettuccine
2 tablespoons fresh parsley, minced

Serves 6.

In a stockpot, bring 8 cups water to a boil.

Meanwhile in a saucepan, heat margarine till hot; add mushrooms and garlic, and saute briefly, about 2 minutes. Stir in asparagus and set aside.

In small bowl, combine egg white and yogurt and mix until smooth. Add milk and Parmesan cheese and stir to mix well. Add pepper and shrimp to sauce and heat through. (Be sure to heat on low flame or setting because yogurt will curdle if too high a heat is used.)

Cook fettuccine according to package directions. Pour sauce over fettuccine and toss to combine. Sprinkle with parsley.

To Freeze: Place individual portions of pasta and sauce in separate vacuum-sealed bags; label and freeze for up to 2 months.

To Serve: Put bags in boiling water, and bring water to a boil again. Boil for 10 to 12 minutes. Add garnishes such as parsley or cheese just before serving.

Per Serving:		Diabetic Exchanges per Serving:	
calories:	300	milk:	0
protein (gm):	19.0	vegetable:	0
fat (gm):	6.1	fruit:	0
cholesterol (mg):	103	bread:	3
sodium (mg):	421	meat:	1
		fat:	0

66

Linguine with Red Clam Sauce

Ingredients you can keep on your pantry shelf make this dish convenient and easy.

2 (6½-oz.) cans minced clams, undrained
1 tablespoon olive oil
2 cloves garlic, minced
1 (14½-oz.) can no-salt-added whole tomatoes, drained and coarsely chopped
2 teaspoons no-salt-added tomato paste
1 teaspoon dried basil
1 teaspoon oregano
8 ozs. linguine, uncooked
4 tablespoons fresh parsley
Serves 4.

Drain clams, reserving juice; set aside.

Heat olive oil in stockpot and add garlic. Saute garlic until tender. Add clam liquid, tomatoes, and tomato paste; bring to boil. Reduce heat; simmer, uncovered, 5 minutes. Remove from heat; stir in clams, basil, and oregano.

Cook linguine until *al dente*. Combine clam sauce and linguine in bowl and sprinkle parsley on top.

2 cups marinara sauce can be used in place of tomatoes.

To Freeze: Place individual portions of pasta and sauce in separate vacuum-sealed bags; label and freeze for up to 2 months.

To Serve: Put bags in boiling water, and bring water to a boil again. Boil 10 to 12 minutes. Add garnishes such as parsley or cheese just before serving.

Per Serving:		Diabetic Exchanges per Serving:	
calories:	267	milk:	0
protein (gm):	15.6	vegetable:	1
fat (gm):	6.2	fruit:	0
cholesterol (mg):	95	bread:	2
sodium (mg):	84	meat:	1
		fat:	1

Pasta Niçoise

Salad:
3 cups freshly cooked pasta, shells or twists
16 ripe olives, pitted and sliced
2 cups green beans, lightly steamed
¼ cup sliced scallions
1 ripe tomato, diced
1 can water-packed white albacore tuna, drained

Dressing:
½ cup parsley, chopped
¼ cup tarragon vinegar
¼ cup water
2 teaspoons canola or safflower oil
1 large clove garlic, crushed
½ teaspoon Dijon mustard
1 teaspoon oregano
Pepper, freshly ground to taste
Serves 4.

Toss pasta with other ingredients and tuna. Put dressing ingredients in a blender, and blend until well mixed. Pour over pasta, toss, and serve.

To Freeze: Place individual portions of pasta and dressing in separate vacuum-sealed bags; label and freeze for up to 2 months.

To Serve: Put bags in boiling water, and bring water to a boil again. Boil 10 to 12 minutes. Add garnishes such as parsley or cheese just before serving.

Per Serving:		Diabetic Exchanges per Serving:	
calories:	245	milk:	0
protein (gm):	17.9	vegetable:	0
fat (gm):	7.1	fruit:	0
cholesterol (mg):	45	bread:	2
sodium (mg):	264	meat:	1
		fat:	1

Pasta with Mushroom Sauce

½ cup dried porcini mushrooms (other dried mushrooms may be used)
1 medium onion, chopped
2 large cloves garlic, minced
2 tablespoons diet margarine
2 tablespoons olive oil
1 cup evaporated skim milk
1 (6-oz.) can tomato paste
1 teaspoon instant chicken bouillon granules
1 teaspoon dried marjoram, crushed
Pepper to taste
1 lb. fettuccine

Serves 6.

Rehydrate mushrooms according to package directions; drain liquid. Cut up any large mushrooms.

Cook mushrooms, onion, and garlic in margarine and olive oil till tender. Stir in milk, tomato paste, bouillon, marjoram, and pepper if desired. Heat through.

Meanwhile, cook fettuccine in boiling water till just tender. Drain. Serve warm pasta topped with mushroom sauce.

To Freeze: Place individual portions of pasta and sauce in separate vacuum-sealed bags; label and freeze for up to 2 months.

To Serve: Put bags in boiling water, and bring water to a boil again. Boil 10 to 12 minutes. Add garnishes such as parsley or cheese just before serving.

Per Serving:		Diabetic Exchanges per Serving:	
calories:	333	milk:	1
protein (gm):	13.5	vegetable:	2
fat (gm):	8.6	fruit:	0
cholesterol (mg):	52	bread:	2
sodium (mg):	249	meat:	0
		fat:	1

Pasta Primavera

¾ lb. pasta
4 tablespoons olive oil
1 lb. package frozen Italian-style vegetables
4 green onions, chopped

1 tablespoon parsley
1 cup cherry tomatoes, cut in half
½ cup Parmesan cheese, freshly grated
Pepper, freshly ground
Serves 6.

Cook pasta in boiling water about 3 minutes. Drain. Toss with 2 tablespoons olive oil.

While pasta cooks, heat 2 tablespoons olive oil in pan, and saute vegetables and onions with parsley and tomatoes. Continue to cook on medium heat about 8 minutes. Add cheese and ground pepper. Toss pasta with sauce.

To Freeze: Place individual portions of pasta and sauce in separate vacuum-sealed bags; label and freeze for up to 2 months.

To Serve: Put bags in boiling water, and bring water to a boil again. Boil 10 to 12 minutes. Add garnishes such as parsley or cheese just before serving.

Per Serving:		Diabetic Exchanges per Serving:	
calories:	317	milk:	0
protein (gm):	11.7	vegetable:	2
fat (gm):	12.8	fruit:	0
cholesterol (mg):	44	bread:	2
sodium (mg):	190	meat:	½
		fat:	2

Spinach and Zucchini Mostaccioli Casserole

10 ozs. uncooked mostaccioli
   (tubular pasta)
1 (10-oz.) package frozen
   chopped spinach, thawed
Vegetable cooking spray
2 teaspoons vegetable oil
1 cup onion, chopped
2 cloves garlic, minced

1 lb. zucchini, cut in 1-in.
   pieces
2 (14½-oz.) cans chunky
   tomatoes, undrained
3 tablespoons tomato paste
1½ teaspoons basil
¾ teaspoon oregano
¼ teaspoon Spike
¼ teaspoon red pepper,
   crushed
½ cup (divided) Parmesan
   cheese, grated
Serves 8.

Cook mostaccioli according to package directions, omitting salt; drain.

Place spinach on paper towels; squeeze until barely moist.

Coat a large non-stick skillet with cooking spray; add oil and place over medium-high heat until hot. Add onion and garlic; saute until tender. Add zucchini; cook until zucchini is just limp, about 4 minutes. Stir in tomatoes and next 5 ingredients; bring to boil. Reduce heat; simmer, uncovered, 5 minutes, stirring occasionally.

Combine pasta, spinach, zucchini mixture, and ¼ cup cheese in bowl; stir well. Spoon into a 13 × 9 × 2-in. baking dish coated with cooking spray. Sprinkle with remaining ¼ cup cheese. Bake at 350° 20 minutes.

To Freeze: Place individual portions of pasta and sauce in separate vacuum-sealed bags; label and freeze for up to 2 months.

To Serve: Put bags in boiling water, and bring water to a boil again. Boil 10 to 12 minutes. Add garnishes such as parsley or cheese just before serving.

Per Serving:		Diabetic Exchanges per Serving:	
calories:	183	milk:	0
protein (gm):	9.4	vegetable:	2
fat (gm):	4.2	fruit:	0
cholesterol (mg):	28	bread:	1
sodium (mg):	318	meat:	1
		fat:	½

Tortellini with Tuna

This dish is great for lunch, a picnic, or light supper.

¾ lb. tortellini (cheese or meat)
1 cup fresh or frozen peas, thawed
½ green bell pepper, chopped
½ cup scallions, chopped
1 (6½-oz.) can tuna, packed in water, drained
1 (14-oz.) can artichoke hearts, drained and quartered
½ cup fresh parsley, chopped
¼ cup fresh basil, chopped

Dressing:
2 tomatoes, diced
2 tablespoons white wine vinegar
2 tablespoons olive oil
2 teaspoons Dijon mustard
1 clove garlic, minced
3 tablespoons scallions, chopped
1 teaspoon oregano
1 teaspoon basil
¼ cup Parmesan cheese
Serves 8.

In a stockpot, cook tortellini until *al dente;* drain and rinse under cold water. Drain thoroughly.

In salad bowl, combine pasta, peas, bell pepper, scallions, tuna, artichokes, parsley, and basil.

Mix dressing ingredients in blender, and blend till smooth. Pour over pasta and toss well. Serve warm or refrigerate and serve cold.

To Freeze: Place individual portions of pasta and dressing in separate vacuum-sealed bags; label and freeze for up to 2 months.

To Serve: Put bags in boiling water, and bring water to a boil again. Boil 10 to 12 minutes. Add garnishes such as parsley or cheese just before serving.

Per Serving:		Diabetic Exchanges per Serving:	
calories:	304	milk:	0
protein (gm):	16.9	vegetable:	1
fat (gm):	14.4	fruit:	0
cholesterol (mg):	29	bread:	1
sodium (mg):	658	meat:	2
		fat:	2

7
RICE IS NICE—
GRAINS ARE GREAT

Perfect Rice

Up to 4 cups of raw rice may be prepared in a crockpot, with a yield of 10 cups cooked. Rub

crockpot lightly with margarine, and add rice and liquid.

2 cups long-grain rice
4 to 6 cups Water, Chicken Stock
  or Beef Stock (see Index)
Makes 5 cups rice.

Place rice and liquid in crockpot, cover, and cook on High 1½ to 2½ hours, stirring occasionally.

When turned off, crockpot will keep rice warm for serving for 2 to 3 hours.

*Note: For quicker brown rice, soak it overnight in water: 1 cup rice to 3 cups water. Then cook it for 20 minutes.

Couscous with Steamed Vegetables

2 cups peas (frozen)
2 cups fresh carrots, thinly sliced
2 cups broccoli florets
2 cups corn (frozen or fresh)

3 cups Chicken Stock (see page 36)
2 cups couscous
¼ cup scallions, sliced
1 cup fresh parsley, chopped
2 tablespoons Parmesan cheese, freshly grated

Serves 8.

Steam peas, carrots, broccoli, and corn in steamer basket until tender. Set aside.

Bring Chicken Stock to boil in stockpot. Slowly stir couscous into stock, then remove pan from heat. Cover tightly and let stand 5 minutes. Stir in scallions and parsley. Pile in center of a serving plate and surround with steamed vegetables. Sprinkle on cheese.

To Freeze: Place individual portions of couscous and vegetables in separate vacuum-sealed bags; label and freeze for up to 2 months.

To Serve: Put bags in boiling water, and bring water to a boil again. Boil 10 to 12 minutes.

Per Serving:		Diabetic Exchanges per Serving:	
calories:	281	milk:	0
protein (gm):	12.8	vegetable:	1
fat (gm):	1.6	fruit:	0
cholesterol (mg):	2	bread:	3½
sodium (mg):	380	meat:	0
		fat:	0

Basic Mushroom Risotto

2 tablespoons diet margarine
2 tablespoons olive oil
½ cup onions, minced
1 cup arborio rice

½ cup mushrooms, sliced
3 cups Chicken Stock (see page 36)
1 teaspoon Spike
Pepper, freshly ground
¼ cup Parmesan cheese, freshly ground

Serves 6.

Heat margarine and olive oil in microwave-safe pie plate on High for 2 minutes. Add onions and stir to coat. Cook, uncovered, on High for 4 minutes. Add rice and mushrooms. Stir to coat. Cook, uncovered, for 4 minutes more. Stir in Chicken Stock. Cook, uncovered, on High for 9 minutes more. Remove from oven.

Let stand, uncovered, for 5 minutes to let rice absorb remaining liquid, stirring several times. Stir in Spike, pepper, and Parmesan cheese.

Per Serving:		**Diabetic Exchanges per Serving:**	
calories:	214	milk:	0
protein (gm):	6.6	vegetable:	½
fat (gm):	8.6	fruit:	0
cholesterol (mg):	3	bread:	1½
sodium (mg):	511	meat:	½
		fat:	1½

Vegetables and Stir-Fried Rice

2 tablespoons vegetable oil
½ cup onions, chopped
¼ cup celery, chopped
¼ cup red bell pepper, chopped
¼ cup yellow bell pepper, chopped
¼ cup green bell pepper, chopped
½ cup water chestnuts, sliced
2 zucchinis, sliced
1 yellow squash, sliced
2 cups pea pods
3 cups Stir-Fried Rice (see next recipe)

Serves 6.

Heat wok and add vegetable oil. Add onion, celery, and peppers. Stir-fry 1 minute. Add water chestnuts. Cover for 45 seconds. Add zucchini, squash, and pea pods. Stir-fry 1 minute. Add Stir-Fried Rice and stir-fry until heated through.

To Freeze: Place individual portions in vacuum-sealed bags; label and freeze for up to 2 months.

To Serve: To reheat, put bags in boiling water, and bring water to a boil again. Boil 10 to 12 minutes. If serving cold, just defrost and use.

Per Serving:		Diabetic Exchanges per Serving:	
calories:	211	milk:	0
protein (gm):	5.0	vegetable:	1
fat (gm):	9.7	fruit:	0
cholesterol (mg):	0	bread:	1½
sodium (mg):	94	meat:	0
		fat:	2

Stir-Fried Rice

1 tablespoon vegetable oil
Egg substitute equal to 1 egg
¼ cup onions, chopped
¼ cup celery, chopped
¼ cup bean sprouts
1 cup mushrooms

2 teaspoons sherry
¼ cup Chicken Stock (see page 36)
3 cups cooked rice
2 teaspoons dark soy sauce
Pepper, dash
¼ teaspoon sugar
2 stalks scallions, chopped
Serves 6.

Heat wok and add oil. Scramble egg substitute in wok. Add onion, celery, bean sprouts, and mushrooms. Add sherry and Chicken Stock, and cover for 45 seconds. Uncover and stir thoroughly. Add soy sauce, pepper, and sugar. Stir thoroughly. Add scallions and rice as you turn flame off. Serve immediately.

Note: ½ cup diced roast pork may be added, or shrimp, to create pork fried rice or shrimp fried rice. Stir-fried vegetables may also be added to create a vegetarian meal.

To Freeze: Place individual portions in vacuum-sealed bags; label and freeze for up to 2 months.

To Serve: To reheat, put bags in boiling water, and bring water to a boil again. Boil 10 to 12 minutes. If serving cold, just defrost and use.

Per Serving:		Diabetic Exchanges per Serving:	
calories:	194	milk:	0
protein (gm):	5.0	vegetable:	½
fat (gm):	5.3	fruit:	0
cholesterol (mg):	0	bread:	2
sodium (mg):	168	meat:	0
		fat:	1

Stuffed Tomatoes

This makes a nice luncheon dish with a green salad, or use as a side dish with beef.

4 large, fresh tomatoes
3 tablespoons vegetable oil
2 medium onions, chopped

1 cup long-grain rice, uncooked
2 cups liquid (tomato pulp and water)
½ cup scallions, sliced
⅓ cup mushrooms, chopped
2 tablespoons breadcrumbs
½ cup tomato juice
Serves 4.

Slice off the top of each tomato, ¾ to 1 in. from the top. Scoop out and reserve pulp and tomato tops.

In a glass measure, microwave oil and onions on High 3½ to 4 minutes or until soft.

Place onions in casserole dish; add rice and tomato pulp and water (combined to make 2 cups). Add scallions and mushrooms, and stir. Microwave, covered with wax paper, on High 5 minutes; reduce to 50 percent power, or Medium, and microwave 15 minutes. Let stand 5 minutes.

Stuff rice mixture into tomato shells and replace tops. Sprinkle with breadcrumbs and add tomato juice.

Microwave, uncovered, on High 4 to 5 minutes or until tomatoes are soft.

To Freeze: Place in microwave-safe casserole; label and freeze for up to 2 months.

To Serve: Thaw. Cover with microwave-safe plastic wrap and cook on High 3 to 5 minutes.

Per Serving:		Diabetic Exchanges per Serving:	
calories:	325	milk:	0
protein (gm):	6.0	vegetable:	2
fat (gm):	11.0	fruit:	0
cholesterol (mg):	0	bread:	2½
sodium (mg):	147	meat:	0
		fat:	2

Tabbouleh

1 cup uncooked bulgur wheat
1 cup cold water
2 cups fresh parsley, minced
1½ cups unpeeled tomatoes
   (about 1 lb.), seeded,
   chopped
1 cup fresh lemon mint,
   minced
½ cup green bell pepper,
   chopped
½ cup unpeel
   seeded, ch
⅓ cup green
2 cloves garlic, mi..
½ cup lemon juice
⅛ teaspoon red pepper,
   ground
⅛ teaspoon black pepper

Serves 10.

Combine bulgur and water in medium bowl; let stand 30 minutes or until water is absorbed. Add parsley and next 6 ingredients, and mix well. Combine remaining ingredients in separate bowl; stir. Drizzle lemon juice over bulgur mixture; toss.

To Freeze: Place individual portions in vacuum-sealed bags; label and freeze for up to 2 months.

To Serve: To reheat, put bags in boiling water, and bring water to a boil again. Boil 10 to 12 minutes. If serving cold, just defrost and use.

Per Serving:		Diabetic Exchanges per Serving:	
calories:	66	milk:	0
protein (gm):	2.6	vegetable:	½
fat (gm):	0.3	fruit:	0
cholesterol (mg):	0	bread:	1
sodium (mg):	11	meat:	0
		fat:	0

8

Here's the Beef

Boeuf Bourguignon

(Beef Stew with Wine)

Vegetable cooking spray
3 lbs. beef rump or chuck, cut into 1½-in. cubes
1 large carrot, peeled and sliced
1 medium onion, sliced
3 tablespoons flour

2 cups Beef Stock (see page 35)
1 tablespoon tomato paste
2 cloves garlic, minced
1 tablespoon thyme
1 teaspoon tarragon
1 bay leaf
½ lb. white onions, peeled, or 1 jar white onions
1 lb. fresh mushrooms, sliced
½ cup red or Burgundy wine
Serves 8.

Heat frying pan and spray with cooking spray. Brown beef, carrots, and onion well. Add flour and Beef Stock. Mix well. Transfer to crockpot. Add tomato paste, garlic, thyme, tarragon, bay leaf, and onions. Cover and cook on Low 8 to 10 hours. Add mushrooms and wine about 1 hour before serving.

To Freeze: Vacuum seal each portion; label and freeze for up to 2 months.

To Serve: Put bags in boiling water, and bring water to a boil again. Boil 10 to 12 minutes.

Per Serving:		Diabetic Exchanges per Serving:	
calories:	328	milk:	0
protein (gm):	39.2	vegetable:	2
fat (gm):	12.7	fruit:	0
cholesterol (mg):	107	bread:	0
sodium (mg):	282	meat:	5
		fat:	0

Veal Lady Sharon

3 tablespoons diet margarine
4 lean loin veal chops
Pepper to taste
2 medium onions, chopped
1 lb. mushrooms, sliced

1 tablespoon flour
1 tablespoon tomato paste
¾ cup Chicken Stock (see page 36)
⅔ cup white wine
1 teaspoon Herbes de Provence
1 small bay leaf
½ cup black olives, sliced
2 tablespoons parsley, minced

Serves 4.

In large stockpot, melt margarine and brown veal chops, seasoned with pepper, quickly. Transfer chops to shallow casserole.

In same stockpot, saute onions. Add remaining ingredients except parsley. Cover and cook 5 minutes.

Pour mixture over chops and bake in preheated 325° oven 1 hour. Sprinkle with parsley and serve.

To Freeze: Place in microwave-safe container; label and freeze for up to 2 months.

To Serve: Thaw, then place in microwave on High 7 to 9 minutes.

Per Serving:		Diabetic Exchanges per Serving:	
calories:	227	milk:	0
protein (gm):	19.1	vegetable:	2
fat (gm):	9.8	fruit:	0
cholesterol (mg):	62	bread:	0
sodium (mg):	365	meat:	2
		fat:	1½

Sukiyaki

4½ cups water, divided
 5 ozs. transparent noodles
  (bean threads), uncooked
¼ cup sugar
 2 tablespoons soy sauce
¼ cup sake (rice wine)
¼ teaspoon beef-flavored
  bouillon granules
 1 lb. lean, boneless sirloin
  steak

1 cup diagonally sliced carrots
2 medium onions, cut into
 thin strips
6 green onions, cut into 1½-
 in. pieces
2 cups fresh mushrooms,
 sliced
4 cups packed Chinese cabbage leaves
1 cup bamboo shoots

Serves 6.

Bring 4 cups water to a boil in a large stockpot; add noodles and cook 2 minutes. Drain. Cut noodles with kitchen shears into 3-in. pieces. Set aside.

Combine ¼ cup water, sugar, soy sauce, sake, and bouillon granules in a bowl. Mix well and set aside.

Partially freeze steak about 20 minutes. Slice it diagonally, across grain, into $\frac{1}{16}$-in. strips. Set aside.

Heat remaining ¼ cup water in a wok. Add beef; stir-fry 2 to 3 minutes. Add ¼ cup soy sauce mixture and carrots; stir-fry 1 minute, stirring frequently. Add onions; stir-fry 3 minutes. Add mushrooms; stir-fry 30 seconds. Add noodles and ¼ cup soy sauce mixture; stir fry 2 minutes. Add Chinese cabbage, bamboo shoots, and remaining soy sauce mixture; toss well. Serve warm.

To Freeze: Place in microwave-safe container; label and freeze for up to 2 months.

To Serve: Thaw, then place in microwave on High 7 to 9 minutes.

Per Serving:		Diabetic Exchanges per Serving:	
calories:	302	milk:	0
protein (gm):	19.8	vegetable:	2
fat (gm):	5.8	fruit:	0
cholesterol (mg):	47	bread:	2
sodium (mg):	448	meat:	2
		fat:	0

60's Meatloaf

½ cup quick-cooking oatmeal,
  uncooked
3 tablespoons skim milk
¾ lb. turkey, ground
¾ lb. chuck, ground
½ cup zucchini, coarsely
  shredded
¼ cup green onions, sliced
¼ teaspoon basil
1 teaspoon garlic powder
¼ teaspoon pepper
1 egg white
Vegetable cooking spray
¼ cup catsup
Serves 8.

Combine oatmeal and milk in a bowl; let stand 10 minutes. Add turkey and next 7 ingredients; stir. Shape into an 8 × 5 × 2-in. loaf. Place on a rack coated with cooking spray; place rack in shallow roasting pan. Brush catsup over loaf.

Bake at 350° for 90 minutes. Let stand 5 minutes before slicing.

To Freeze: Place in microwave-safe container; label and freeze for up to 2 months.

To Serve: Thaw and slice. Place in microwave on High 7 to 9 minutes.

Per Serving:		Diabetic Exchanges per Serving:	
calories:	149	milk:	0
protein (gm):	13.7	vegetable:	0
fat (gm):	6.4	fruit:	0
cholesterol (mg):	37	bread:	½
sodium (mg):	132	meat:	2
		fat:	0

Speedy Chili

2 teaspoons olive oil
2 lbs. beef, ground
2 lbs. turkey, ground
2 large onions, chopped
3 cloves garlic, minced
½ teaspoon pepper, ground

1 can (6 oz.) tomato paste
2 cans (10½ oz.) zesty tomato sauce
2 cans (15½ oz.) kidney beans
2 tablespoons chili powder
1 teaspoon oregano
2 tablespoons fresh parsley, chopped

Serves 8.

Place ground beef and turkey in stockpot with oil. Add onions and garlic and saute until meat is browned. Add remaining ingredients (except parsley) and bring to a boil. Reduce heat to simmer, and simmer 15 minutes. Spoon into serving tureen and top with parsley.

To Freeze: Vacuum seal each portion; label and freeze for up to 2 months.

To Serve: Thaw in the refrigerator or in a bowl of water. Serve chilled.

Per Serving:		Diabetic Exchanges per Serving:	
calories:	304	milk:	0
protein (gm):	26.6	vegetable:	1
fat (gm):	15.6	fruit:	0
cholesterol (mg):	77	bread:	1
sodium (mg):	483	meat:	3
		fat:	1

Swiss Steak

1½ lbs. round steak, ½-in. thick
1 teaspoon instant meat tenderizer
¼ cup flour

1½ teaspoons Spike
1 teaspoon garlic powder
1 medium onion, sliced thin
1 can (16 oz.) tomatoes
½ cup mushrooms, sliced
Serves 6.

Pound steak with mallet until about ¼-in. thick. Cut meat into 6 pieces. Sprinkle with tenderizer, then coat with mixture of flour, Spike, and garlic powder. Place in 3-qt. casserole. Cover with onion.

Break up tomatoes with fork and pour over top. Add mushrooms and stir. Cover dish and place in microwave oven. Cook 12 minutes on High. Rearrange meat so bottom pieces are on top. Cover and continue cooking 10 to 12 minutes or until tender.

To Freeze: Place in microwave-safe casserole; label and freeze for up to 2 months.

To Serve: Thaw. Cover with microwave-safe plastic wrap, and cook on High 3 to 5 minutes.

Per Serving:		Diabetic Exchanges per Serving:	
calories:	217	milk:	0
protein (gm):	25.7	vegetable:	1
fat (gm):	8.4	fruit:	0
cholesterol (mg):	70	bread:	0
sodium (mg):	175	meat:	3
		fat:	0

Imperial Tomato, Corn & Beef Salad

I like to make this salad after cooking the Pot Roast of Beef (recipe follows). I always have enough left over for 2 more meals, and this is one of them.

8 firm, ripe tomatoes, peeled
1 cup frozen corn kernels, cooked
1 lb. beef, cooked, cut diagonally across the grain into ¼-in.-thick slices and then cut crosswise into ½-in. strips
½ cup parsley, chopped
1 clove garlic, minced
1 teaspoon Spike
1 teaspoon sugar
¼ teaspoon pepper
¼ cup olive oil
2 tablespoons tarragon or wine vinegar
2 teaspoons Dijon mustard
1 green bell pepper cut into rings
8 cups mixed salad greens

Serves 8.

Cut stem ends from tomatoes and slice. Place tomatoes, corn, and beef in a shallow dish.

Combine remaining ingredients, except greens, in blender. Blend 30 seconds and pour over beef mixture. Refrigerate until ready to serve.

To serve: Place greens in a large salad bowl and top with beef mixture. Toss well and serve on individual salad plates.

To Freeze: Vacuum seal beef mixture in individual portions; label and freeze for up to 2 months.

To Serve: Thaw beef mixture. Place greens in a large salad bowl and top with beef mixture.

Per Serving:		Diabetic Exchanges per Serving:	
calories:	134	milk:	0
protein (gm):	4.9	vegetable:	2
fat (gm):	8.0	fruit:	0
cholesterol (mg):	6	bread:	0
sodium (mg):	40	meat:	1
		fat:	1

Pot Roast of Beef

3 potatoes, pared and sliced
3 carrots, pared and sliced
2 onions, peeled and sliced

2 ribs of celery with tops, sliced
3–4 lb. brisket or pot roast
Pepper to taste
½ cup Beef Stock (see page 35)
Serves 6.

Put vegetables in crockpot. Season meat with pepper and place in pot. Add Beef Stock. Cover and cook on Low 10 to 12 hours or on High 4 to 5 hours. Remove meat and vegetables with a spatula.

To Freeze: Place in microwave-safe container; label and freeze for up to 2 months.

To Serve: Thaw, then place in microwave on High 7 to 9 minutes.

Note: Freezing and Serving instructions are the same for the six variations that follow.

Per Serving:		Diabetic Exchanges per Serving:	
calories:	599	milk:	0
protein (gm):	71.5	vegetable:	1
fat (gm):	23.5	fruit:	0
cholesterol (mg):	203	bread:	1
sodium (mg):	241	meat:	9
		fat:	0

POT ROAST OF BEEF VARIATIONS (all serve 6)

German Style: Add 3 or 4 medium dill pickles, 1 teaspoon dill weed, and 1 tablespoon wine vinegar.

Per Serving:		Diabetic Exchanges per Serving:	
calories:	602	milk:	0
protein (gm):	71.6	vegetable:	1½
fat (gm):	23.5	fruit:	0
cholesterol (mg):	203	bread:	1
sodium (mg):	705	meat:	9
		fat:	0

Italian Style: Add 1 cup of tomato sauce, 1 teaspoon oregano, and 1 teaspoon basil.

Per Serving:		Diabetic Exchanges per Serving:	
calories:	612	milk:	0
protein (gm):	72.1	vegetable:	2
fat (gm):	23.6	fruit:	0
cholesterol (mg):	203	bread:	1
sodium (mg):	493	meat:	9
		fat:	0

Chinese Style: Add white part of 4 medium green onions, 2 tablespoons chopped fresh ginger root, 1 tablespoon minced garlic, 1 cup water, 3 tablespoons soy sauce. Garnish with the peel of 1 orange.

Per Serving:		Diabetic Exchanges per Serving:	
calories:	621	milk:	0
protein (gm):	73.4	vegetable:	2
fat (gm):	23.7	fruit:	0
cholesterol (mg):	203	bread:	1
sodium (mg):	921	meat:	9
		fat:	0

Mexican Style: Add ½ cup chopped green onion, 1 tablespoon minced garlic, 1 cup beef broth mixed with 2 tablespoons tomato paste, and ¼ cup chili powder. Garnish with ¼ cup raisins.

Per Serving:		Diabetic Exchanges per Serving:	
calories:	655	milk:	0
protein (gm):	74.1	vegetable:	2
fat (gm):	24.8	fruit:	½
cholesterol (mg):	203	bread:	1
sodium (mg):	596	meat:	9
		fat:	0

Scandinavian Style: Add 1 cup thinly sliced onions, 12 oz. beef or 1¼ cups beef stock, 2 tablespoons cider vinegar, and 2 tablespoons sugar. Garnish with fresh dill.

Per Serving:		Diabetic Exchanges per Serving:	
calories:	629	milk:	0
protein (gm):	72.4	vegetable:	2
fat (gm):	23.7	fruit:	0
cholesterol (mg):	203	bread:	1
sodium (mg):	407	meat:	9
		fat:	0

French Style: Add 1 cup fresh sliced mushrooms, 1 lb. small peeled onions, and 1 cup red wine.

Per Serving:		Diabetic Exchanges per Serving:	
calories:	640	milk:	0
protein (gm):	72.2	vegetable:	2
fat (gm):	23.6	fruit:	0
cholesterol (mg):	203	bread:	1
sodium (mg):	268	meat:	9
		fat:	½

9
On the Lamb

Irish Stew

1½ lbs. shoulder of lamb, cut
    into 1-in. cubes
6 white potatoes, thinly sliced
6 white onions

2½ teaspoons Spike
2 teaspoons rosemary
½ teaspoon thyme
6 carrots, sliced
1 bay leaf
2 cups water
Serves 6.

Place lamb, potatoes, and onions in crockpot. Sprinkle with Spike, rosemary, and thyme. Place carrots in pot and mix well. Add bay leaf and water. Cover and cook on High 1 hour; turn to Low and cook additional 10 to 12 hours.

To Freeze: Vacuum seal individual portions; label and freeze for up to 2 months.

To Serve: Put bags in boiling water, and bring to a boil again. Boil 10 to 12 minutes.

Per Serving:		Diabetic Exchanges per Serving:	
calories:	304	milk:	0
protein (gm):	21.8	vegetable:	1
fat (gm):	8.3	fruit:	0
cholesterol (mg):	64	bread:	1½
sodium (mg):	83	meat:	3
		fat:	0

Lamb- Stuffed Cabbage Rolls

1 red or white cabbage (about
  2½ to 3 lbs.)
1 onion, minced
1 tablespoon safflower oil
1 teaspoon curry powder

1 lb. lean ground lamb (beef
  may be substituted)
½ cup dry whole-wheat
  breadcrumbs
1 egg white
½ teaspoon black pepper,
  ground
¼ teaspoon coriander, ground
1 (8-oz.) can tomato sauce
Serves 6.

Remove and discard any discolored cabbage leaves and cut out core. Rinse cored cabbage and place on rack over boiling water. Cover and steam 5 minutes. Remove leaves with tongs until you have 12 leaves. Cut out thick part of rib along base of each leaf. Set aside.

Mix together remaining ingredients for filling (except tomato sauce) and place in microwave bowl. Microwave on High 4 minutes.

Place 2 to 2½ tablespoons of filling on each leaf, roll one turn, tuck in sides, and continue to roll. Place rolls, seam side down, on plate. Set aside.

Shred remaining cabbage and place in shallow dish. Arrange cabbage rolls in circular pattern over the cabbage. Place dish on rack over boiling water, cover pot, and steam 20 to 25 minutes. Serve with tomato sauce.

To Freeze: Place in microwave-safe casserole; label and freeze for up to 2 months.

To Serve: Thaw. Cover with microwave-safe plastic wrap, and cook on High 3 to 5 minutes.

Per Serving:		Diabetic Exchanges per Serving:	
calories:	209	milk:	0
protein (gm):	18.0	vegetable:	3
fat (gm):	8.5	fruit:	0
cholesterol (mg):	43	bread:	0
sodium (mg):	597	meat:	2
		fat:	½

Moussaka

3 medium-size eggplants,
    peeled
1 cup onions, finely chopped
¾ cup olive oil (divided)
2 lbs. lean ground lamb
1 cup drained canned or fresh
    tomatoes, or 3 tablespoons
    tomato paste

⅓ cup parsley, chopped
1 cup white wine
¼ teaspoon nutmeg
Black pepper, freshly ground
3 egg whites
½ cup fine breadcrumbs
Serves 10.

Slice eggplants lengthwise into slices ¼ to ½-in. thick. Place in colander and set aside.

Meanwhile, saute onions and ground lamb in ¼ cup olive oil. Add tomatoes, parsley, and white wine and simmer gently about 45 minutes. Add nutmeg and black pepper.

Quickly saute eggplant in ½ cup olive oil until lightly browned on all sides.

Beat 3 egg whites until stiff but not dry, and fold beaten whites with breadcrumbs into cooked and cooled meat mixture.

Assemble ingredients in a 9 × 13-in. microwave dish, layering eggplant, meat, and eggplant again. Microwave on High 25 minutes.

To Freeze: Place in microwave-safe casserole; label and freeze for up to 2 months.

To Serve: Thaw. Cover with microwave-safe plastic wrap, and cook on High 3 to 5 minutes.

Per Serving:		Diabetic Exchanges per Serving:	
calories:	275	milk:	1
protein (gm):	19.2	vegetable:	0
fat (gm):	14.9	fruit:	0
cholesterol (mg):	58	bread:	0
sodium (mg):	271	meat:	2
		fat:	2

10

PORK **F**UTURES

Cantonese Pork Dinner

1½ lbs. pork steak, ½-in. thick, cut into strips
2 tablespoons vegetable oil
1 large onion, sliced
1 red bell pepper, cut into strips

1 cup fresh mushrooms
1 can (8 oz.) tomato sauce
3 tablespoons brown sugar
1½ tablespoons vinegar
2 teaspoons Worcestershire sauce
1 tablespoon sherry
3 cups cooked rice
Serves 6.

Brown pork strips in oil to remove excess fat. Drain on paper towels. Place pork strips and remaining ingredients in crockpot and cover. Cook on Low 6 to 8 hours or High 4 hours. Serve over rice.

To Freeze: Vacuum seal each portion; label and freeze for up to 2 months.

To Serve: Put bags in boiling water, and bring water to a boil again. Boil 10 to 12 minutes.

Per Serving:		Diabetic Exchanges per Serving:	
calories:	293	milk:	0
protein (gm):	22.4	vegetable:	2
fat (gm):	16.4	fruit:	0
cholesterol (mg):	72	bread:	0
sodium (mg):	323	meat:	3½
		fat:	1

Sweet-and-Sour Pork

2 teaspoons vegetable oil
½ cup red bell pepper, cut in strips
¼ cup scallions, sliced
¼ cup carrots, shredded
2 garlic cloves, minced

1 lb. pork, cut into cubes
½ cup Chicken Stock (see page 36)
2 teaspoons red wine vinegar
2 teaspoons soy sauce
1 teaspoon brown sugar, firmly packed
1 tablespoon water
2 teaspoons cornstarch
½ cup pineapple chunks (no sugar added)
Serves 4.

In wok, heat oil. Add pepper, scallions, carrots, and garlic. Saute until vegetables are tender-crisp, about 5 minutes. Stir in pork cubes, Chicken Stock, vinegar, soy sauce, and brown sugar. Bring to boil, and reduce heat, and let simmer 5 minutes.

In small bowl, combine water and cornstarch, stirring to dissolve cornstarch. Add to wok, along with pineapple, and cook, stirring constantly, until mixture is thickened. Serve over rice.

To Freeze: Vacuum seal each portion; label and freeze for up to 2 months.

To Serve: Put bags in boiling water, and bring water to a boil again. Boil 10 to 12 minutes.

Per Serving:		Diabetic Exchanges per Serving:	
calories:	343	milk:	0
protein (gm):	35.1	vegetable:	0
fat (gm):	18.0	fruit:	0
cholesterol (mg):	107	bread:	1
sodium (mg):	356	meat:	5
		fat:	½

Pork and Vegetable Stir-Fry

1 lb. boneless pork
4 teaspoons cornstarch
4 tablespoons sherry or white wine
8 tablespoons vegetable oil
2 cloves garlic
3 teaspoons fresh ginger root, minced

4 cups broccoli florets
2 zucchini, sliced ½-in. wide
¼ cup carrot, grated

Seasoning Sauce:
4 tablespoons water
4 tablespoons sherry or white wine
2 teaspoons cornstarch
2 teaspoons soy sauce

Serves 4.

Cut meat into thin strips, about 2 in. long.

In a bowl, mix cornstarch and sherry, stir in meat, and let stand 10 minutes or longer until marinated (up to 2 hours).

In small bowl, combine Seasoning Sauce ingredients and mix well.

In wok, heat oil over high heat. Add garlic, ginger, and meat; stir-fry 1 minute. Add broccoli, zucchini, and carrot and stir-fry 2 minutes or until crisp-tender; add water if necessary to prevent scorching. Stir in seasoning sauce and stir-fry another minute.

To Freeze: Vacuum seal each portion; label and freeze for up to 2 months.

To Serve: Put bags in boiling water, and bring water to a boil again. Boil 10 to 12 minutes.

Per Serving:		Diabetic Exchanges per Serving:	
calories:	520	milk:	0
protein (gm):	23.0	vegetable:	2
fat (gm):	39.0	fruit:	0
cholesterol (mg):	73	bread:	0
sodium (mg):	259	meat:	3
		fat:	7

Pork Chop Delight

6 pork chops
Pepper
Spike
2 medium-sweet potatoes, or
 substitute white potatoes

1 large onion, sliced
2 small apples, cubed
3 tablespoons brown sugar
1 large green bell pepper
1 teaspoon oregano
1 teaspoon thyme
2 cups apple cider
Serves 6.

Trim fat from pork chops, season with pepper and Spike. Brown in skillet to remove excess fat, about 10 minutes. Drain and place in crockpot. Add remaining ingredients in order listed. Cover and cook on Low 8 to 10 hours or on High 3 to 4 hours.

To Freeze: Vacuum seal each portion; label and freeze for up to 2 months.

To Serve: Put bags in boiling water, and bring water to a boil again. Boil 10 to 12 minutes.

Per Serving:		Diabetic Exchanges per Serving:	
calories:	304	milk:	0
protein (gm):	19.5	vegetable:	0
fat (gm):	10.4	fruit:	1
cholesterol (mg):	63	bread:	1
sodium (mg):	56	meat:	3
		fat:	0

Roast Pork Chops Calypso

4 center-cut pork chops
½ teaspoon pepper
1 teaspoon Spike
1 teaspoon ginger, ground
½ teaspoon cloves, ground

2 cloves garlic, minced
2 bayleaves, crumbled
1 cup dark rum
2½ cups Chicken Stock (see page 36)
½ cup brown sugar
⅓ cup lime juice
2 teaspoons arrowroot
Zest of 1 lime
Serves 4.

Place chops in shallow baking dish. Add remaining ingredients and bake at 325° for 50 to 60 minutes, basting frequently. Keep stirring until gravy has thickened.

To Freeze: Place in microwave-safe container; label and freeze for up to 2 months.

To Serve: Thaw, then microwave on High 7 to 9 minutes.

Per Serving:		Diabetic Exchanges per Serving:	
calories:	434	milk:	0
protein (gm):	21.5	vegetable:	0
fat (gm):	10.9	fruit:	0
cholesterol (mg):	63	bread:	2
sodium (mg):	542	meat:	2
		fat:	3

Pot-Roasted Pork

4- to 5-lb. boneless pork roast
1 tablespoon rosemary
1 teaspoon cracked pepper

1 clove garlic, sliced
2 medium onions, sliced
2 bay leaves
1 whole clove
1 cup hot water
2 tablespoons white wine
Serves 6.

Rub pork roast with rosemary and pepper. Make tiny slits in meat and insert slivers of garlic. Place roast in broiler pan and broil 15 minutes to remove excess fat.

Put 1 sliced onion in bottom of crockpot. Add browned pork roast and remaining onion, along with other ingredients. Cover and cook on Low until done, about 10 hours.

Note: To thicken gravy, first remove roast to serving platter. Blend 2 tablespoons cornstarch with 2 tablespoons water to form smooth paste. Set crockpot on High and pour in paste. Stir well and let come to boil, about 15 minutes, until thickened.

To Freeze: Place in microwave-safe container; label and freeze for up to 2 months.

To Serve: Thaw. Microwave on High 12 to 14 minutes.

Per Serving:		Diabetic Exchanges per Serving:	
calories:	291	milk:	0
protein (gm):	33.9	vegetable:	0
fat (gm):	15.4	fruit:	0
cholesterol (mg):	107	bread:	0
sodium (mg):	83	meat:	5
		fat:	0

Cuban Pork Sandwiches

2 tablespoons olive oil
2 large onions, sliced thin
⅓ cup fresh cilantro, chopped
¼ teaspoon pepper

1 cup gravy
1 lb. cooked pork, sliced
4 soft hero rolls (6-in. long),
    cut lengthwise in half
4 slices tomato, cut in half
4 large black olives, sliced
Pimiento, diced, for garnish
    (optional)
Serves 4.

Heat oil in stockpot over medium heat. Add onions and cook 10 to 15 minutes, stirring several times until golden. Add cilantro and pepper. Stir well. Put onion mixture in small bowl and set aside.

In same pot, heat gravy over medium-low heat. When gravy is hot, add pork slices and heat through.

Place rolls, cut sides up, on individual plates. Arrange pork slices on rolls. Top with onion mixture. Pour gravy over sandwiches and garnish with tomato, olives, and pimiento.

To Freeze: Add onion mixture to meat and vacuum seal individual portions. Vacuum seal gravy separately. Label and freeze for up to 2 months.

To Serve: Place bags in boiling water, and bring water to a boil again. Boil 10 to 12 minutes. Arrange pork slices on fresh rolls. Divide gravy among sandwiches.

Per Serving:		Diabetic Exchanges per Serving:	
calories:	592	milk:	0
protein (gm):	41.3	vegetable:	1
fat (gm):	25.6	fruit:	0
cholesterol (mg):	108	bread:	2½
sodium (mg):	794	meat:	5
		fat:	3

11
FOWL IS FAIR

Award Winning Chicken

1 tablespoon olive oil
4 boneless, skinless chicken
  breast halves

Pepper, freshly ground
½ cup onion, chopped
¼ cup green bell pepper,
  chopped
Sauce of your choice—recipes
  follow
Serves 4.

Heat olive oil in stockpot over medium-high heat. Add chicken breast halves, and sprinkle with freshly ground pepper. Cook until golden, about 4 to 5 minutes per side.

Add chopped onion and green bell pepper and cook until tender, about 3 to 4 minutes.

Add your choice of sauce to pot (sauce recipes follow) and cook about 3 to 5 minutes. Serve sauce over chicken breasts and top with garnish.

To Freeze: Vacuum seal individual portions; label and freeze for up to 2 months.

To Serve: Put bags in boiling water, and bring water to a boil again. Boil 10 to 12 minutes.

Per Serving:		Diabetic Exchanges per Serving:	
calories:	180	milk:	0
protein (gm):	27.0	vegetable:	½
fat (gm):	6.5	fruit:	0
cholesterol (mg):	73	bread:	0
sodium (mg):	63	meat:	3
		fat:	½

SAUCES FOR AWARD WINNING CHICKEN (all serve 4)*

Greek Style	1 tablespoon grated lemon peel
¾ cup Chicken Stock (see page 36)	1 teaspoon oregano
2 tablespoons lemon juice	8 sliced olives for garnish
	Serves 4.

Place all ingredients (except garnish) in small saucepan and heat until hot; do not boil.

To Freeze: Vacuum seal individual portions; label and freeze for up to 2 months.

To Serve: Put bags in boiling water, and bring water to a boil again. Boil 10 to 12 minutes.

Per Serving:		**Diabetic Exchanges per Serving:**	
calories:	20	milk:	0
protein (gm):	1.2	vegetable:	0
fat (gm):	1.6	fruit:	0
cholesterol (mg):	0	bread:	0
sodium (mg):	184	meat:	0
		fat:	½

Note: *Preparation, Freezing, and Serving instructions are the same as above for all four variations that follow.*

French Style	1 jar pearl onions
⅓ cup Chicken Stock (see Index)	1 teaspoon thyme
⅓ cup red wine	4 tablespoons minced, fresh parsley for garnish
½ lb. mushrooms	

Per Serving:		**Diabetic Exchanges per Serving:**	
calories:	30	milk:	0
protein (gm):	1.9	vegetable:	1
fat (gm):	0.4	fruit:	0
cholesterol (mg):	0	bread:	0
sodium (mg):	81	meat:	0
		fat:	0

Italian Style
½ cup low-fat yogurt
1 tablespoon basil
1 small chopped tomato

1 tablespoon oregano
Dash freshly ground pepper
4 anchovies or fresh parsley for
  garnish

Per Serving:		Diabetic Exchanges per Serving:	
calories:	32	milk:	½
protein (gm):	2.9	vegetable:	0
fat (gm):	0.9	fruit:	0
cholesterol (mg):	5	bread:	0
sodium (mg):	169	meat:	0
		fat:	0

Mexican Style
¾ cup Chicken Stock (see
  Index)
1 jalapeño pepper, minced
1 teaspoon chili powder

⅓ cup low-fat yogurt
1 small diced tomato
2 tablespoons chopped cilantro
  for garnish

Per Serving:		Diabetic Exchanges per Serving:	
calories:	25	milk:	0
protein (gm):	2.1	vegetable:	1
fat (gm):	0.6	fruit:	0
cholesterol (mg):	1	bread:	0
sodium (mg):	192	meat:	0
		fat:	0

Chinese Style
⅓ cup Chicken Stock (see
  Index)
½ lb. mushrooms

½ cup water chestnuts, sliced
4 scallions, sliced
3 tablespoons sesame seeds for
  garnish

Per Serving:		Diabetic Exchanges per Serving:	
calories:	66	milk:	0
protein (gm):	3.0	vegetable:	1
fat (gm):	3.7	fruit:	0
cholesterol (mg):	0	bread:	0
sodium (mg):	68	meat:	0
		fat:	1

Basic Chicken with Herbs

This is a great basic chicken recipe that can be used to make salads or other dishes that require cooked chicken.

1 chicken, 3 to 4 lbs., cut into serving parts (use all white meat if you prefer)

¼ cup dry white wine
3 to 4 garlic cloves, minced
1 tablespoon tarragon
1 tablespoon basil
1 teaspoon thyme
1 teaspoon oregano
1 teaspoon black pepper, freshly ground
3 green onions with tops
Parsley sprigs, fresh
Serves 8.

Place chicken parts in shallow bowl. Pour wine over and sprinkle with garlic, herbs, and pepper. Place green onions and some parsley on top of chicken, and set bowl on rack over boiling water in steamer. Cover pot and steam 45 minutes or until juices run clear when pierced with fork. The more crowded the pieces, the longer it will take to cook.

To Freeze: Place in microwave-safe casserole; label and freeze for up to 2 months.

To Serve: Thaw. Cover with microwave-safe plastic wrap, and cook on High 3 to 5 minutes.

Per Serving:		Diabetic Exchanges per Serving:	
calories:	362	milk:	0
protein (gm):	30.5	vegetable:	0
fat (gm):	24.8	fruit:	0
cholesterol (mg):	108	bread:	0
sodium (mg):	92	meat:	4
		fat:	2½

Chicken Breasts in Champagne Sauce

3 tablespoons all-purpose flour
2 tablespoons garlic powder
2 tablespoons oregano
2 whole chicken breasts,
  boned, skinned, and split

2 tablespoons olive oil
1 lb. mushrooms, sliced
2 tablespoons diet margarine
2 tablespoons all-purpose flour
1 can (12 oz.) evaporated skim milk
½ cup champagne
2 tablespoons parsley, chopped
Serves 4.

Mix together flour, garlic powder, and oregano in paper bag. Shake chicken in bag to coat; shake off any excess. Heat olive oil in stockpot on low heat. Lightly brown chicken on both sides over medium heat. Add sliced mushrooms, cover, and cook 25 minutes. Remove chicken and mushrooms from pot with slotted spoon; keep warm. Pour off liquid and wipe pot clean.

Melt margarine in same pot over low heat. Add 2 tablespoons flour and cook 3 minutes. Do not brown. Remove from heat and slowly add evaporated skim milk, stirring constantly with spoon. Cook and stir over low heat 10 minutes. Sauce will be thick. Add champagne to sauce. Cook, stirring constantly, over low heat 5 minutes.

Add chicken breasts and mushrooms to sauce, and continue cooking till heated through.

Garnish with parsley.

To Freeze: Vacuum seal individual portions; label and freeze for up to 2 months.

To Serve: Put bags in boiling water, and bring water to a boil again. Boil 10 to 12 minutes.

Per Serving:		Diabetic Exchanges per Serving:	
calories:	408	milk:	1
protein (gm):	38.3	vegetable:	1
fat (gm):	13.5	fruit:	0
cholesterol (mg):	77	bread:	½
sodium (mg):	244	meat:	3
		fat:	2

Chicken Gumbo

9 ozs. cooked chicken (can be canned, frozen, or roasted)
2½ cups Chicken Stock (see page 36) or 2 cans (10½ oz. each) chicken broth
1 cup onion, diced
2 cloves garlic, minced
1 can (14½ oz.) stewed tomatoes, undrained

10 ozs. fresh or frozen okra
¼ cup red or green bell pepper, chopped
1 teaspoon basil
¼ teaspoon red pepper flakes
1 teaspoon thyme
¼ teaspoon pepper
3 cups cooked rice

Serves 6.

Combine chicken and Chicken Stock in stockpot; bring to boil. Cover, reduce heat, and simmer 3 minutes. Add remaining ingredients; bring to boil. Cover, reduce heat, and simmer 10 minutes. To serve, ladle gumbo over ½ cup rice.

To Freeze: Place in microwave-safe casserole; label and freeze for up to 2 months.

To Serve: Thaw. Cover with microwave-safe plastic wrap, and cook on High 3 to 5 minutes.

Per Serving:		Diabetic Exchanges per Serving:	
calories:	254	milk:	0
protein (gm):	19.7	vegetable:	1½
fat (gm):	2.7	fruit:	0
cholesterol (mg):	36	bread:	1½
sodium (mg):	471	meat:	2
		fat:	0

Coq au Vin

1 2½-lb. broiler-fryer, cut up and skinned (or 3 skinned chicken breasts, halved, or 3 drumsticks and 3 thighs)
⅔ cup green onions, chopped
8 small white onions, peeled
½ lb. whole fresh mushrooms
1 clove garlic, crushed
1 teaspoon Spike
¼ teaspoon pepper
½ teaspoon thyme
8 small new potatoes, scrubbed
1 cup Chicken Stock (see page 36)
Parsley, chopped
1 cup Burgundy wine

Serves 6.

In a stockpot, saute green onions and chicken until chicken is browned on all sides. Add chicken and onions to crockpot with small white onions, mushrooms, garlic, Spike, pepper, thyme, potatoes, Chicken Stock and parsley. Cook on Low 8 to 10 hours. During last hour, add Burgundy.

To Freeze: Place in microwave-safe casserole; label and freeze for up to 2 months.

To Serve: Thaw in refrigerator; garnish before serving if desired.

Per Serving:		Diabetic Exchanges per Serving:	
calories:	374	milk:	0
protein (gm):	46.8	vegetable:	½
fat (gm):	5.4	fruit:	0
cholesterol (mg):	117	bread:	1½
sodium (mg):	262	meat:	5
		fat:	0

Simmered Chicken

1 chicken, quartered (about 4½ lbs.)
2 large stalks celery, with tops, cut in half
1 large carrot, halved

1 medium-size onion, halved
1 teaspoon Spike
5 peppercorns
1 teaspoon thyme
1 tablespoon fresh parsley, minced
4 cups water
Serves 8.

Place all ingredients in stockpot and bring to boil. Lower heat; cover and simmer 30 to 40 minutes until chicken is tender. Remove chicken; cool. Skim broth if necessary. Strain into container; cool to room temperature. Cover and refrigerate until cold. Remove fat from surface before using.

Skin chicken. Remove meat from breast in one piece, and cut remaining portions into bite-size pieces. Refrigerate in covered containers separately from broth.

You should have 1½ lbs. boneless chicken meat and 5 cups broth.

To Freeze: Place in microwave-safe casserole; label and freeze for up to 2 months.

To Serve: Thaw. Cover with microwave-safe plastic wrap, and cook on High 3 to 5 minutes.

Per Serving:		Diabetic Exchanges per Serving:	
calories:	203	milk:	0
protein (gm):	24.8	vegetable:	0
fat (gm):	9.9	fruit:	0
cholesterol (mg):	73	bread:	0
sodium (mg):	53	meat:	4
		fat:	0

Chicken Veronique

2 whole, large chicken breasts
2 tablespoons vegetable oil
1 cup fresh mushrooms, sliced
3 tablespoons green onions, sliced
1 cup Chicken Stock (see p. 36)

1 tablespoon all-purpose flour
1 cup seedless green grapes, halved
¼ cup dry white wine
1 tablespoon capers
2 cups cooked rice
Serves 4.

Bone chicken breasts, and cut meat into 1-in. pieces; set aside.

In wok, heat vegetable oil and stir-fry mushrooms and onions about 2 minutes or until soft. Add chicken pieces and stir-fry about 5 minutes or until chicken is white.

Blend Chicken Stock and flour; add to chicken mixture. Cook and stir till thickened and bubbly. Stir in grapes, wine, and capers; cook 1 minute longer. Spoon chicken over rice in bowl.

To Freeze: Vacuum seal individual portions; label and freeze for up to 2 months.

To Serve: Put bags in boiling water, and bring to a boil again. Boil 10 to 12 minutes.

Per Serving:		Diabetic Exchanges per Serving:	
calories:	339	milk:	0
protein (gm):	30.6	vegetable:	½
fat (gm):	6.5	fruit:	0
cholesterol (mg):	73	bread:	2
sodium (mg):	205	meat:	3
		fat:	½

Poached Turkey Breast with Herbs & Wine

1 cup parsley, chopped
1 tablespoon garlic, minced
2 tablespoons lemon juice
1 tablespoon olive oil
1 4- to 5-lb., bone-in turkey
  breast, ready to cook
1 sprig sorrel leaves
3 thin slices carrot

1 cup Chicken Stock (see page 36)
1 cup white wine
4 medium red-skinned potatoes
4 large carrots, peeled and cut
  into 2-in. pieces
1 cup green beans, cut in half
1 cup zucchini, sliced
6 cherry tomatoes and fresh basil leaves for garnish
Meal No. 1
Serves 4.

Put parsley, garlic, lemon juice, and olive oil in blender and blend till smooth.

Gently run spoon under turkey skin to separate from flesh, leaving skin attached at one end. Spread parsley mixture over breast, and arrange sorrel leaves and carrot slices in decorative pattern. Replace skin and secure with skewer to hold herbs against turkey.

Place turkey, skin side up, in large stockpot. Add Chicken Stock and wine. Bring to boil over medium-high heat. Reduce heat to low, cover, and simmer 1 hour. Scatter potatoes and carrots around turkey and cover. Simmer 15 minutes. Add green beans and zucchini, and simmer 10 minutes more or until potatoes and carrots are tender and meat juices run clear when breast is pierced.

Place turkey on cutting board and let stand 10 minutes, loosely covered with foil. Remove vegetables from broth and place around edge of serving platter.

To serve: Remove skewers from turkey and discard skin. Carve ⅓ of breast and add to platter with vegetables. Cut ⅓ more breast into slices and freeze in a bag for meal No. 2 (see p. 111).

Pour ⅓ of broth over turkey to moisten, and garnish with tomatoes and basil leaves.

To Freeze: Place in microwave-safe casserole; label and freeze for up to 2 months.

To Serve: Thaw. Cover with microwave-safe plastic wrap, and cook on High 3 to 5 minutes.

Per Serving:		Diabetic Exchanges per Serving:	
calories:	313	milk:	0
protein (gm):	53.0	vegetable:	1
fat (gm):	2.6	fruit:	0
cholesterol (mg):	142	bread:	½
sodium (mg):	179	meat:	5
		fat:	0

Poached Turkey 'n Dressing

1 herb-seasoned stuffing mix (8 oz.)
½ cup celery

¼ cup onion
2 tablespoons pimiento, chopped
1½ cups Chicken Stock (see page 36)
Turkey slices (from meal No. 1)
Meal No. 2
Serves 4.

Toss together stuffing mix, celery, onion, pimiento, and Chicken Stock in 3-quart, microwave-safe casserole. Place dish in microwave oven and cook 18 minutes, giving dish half-turn after 9 minutes. Add turkey slices and cook 3 more minutes.

To Freeze: Place in microwave-safe casserole; label and freeze for up to 2 months.

To Serve: Thaw. Cover with microwave-safe plastic wrap, and cook on High 3 to 5 minutes.

Per Serving:		Diabetic Exchanges per Serving:	
calories:	369	milk:	0
protein (gm):	56.3	vegetable:	1
fat (gm):	3.6	fruit:	0
cholesterol (mg):	142	bread:	1
sodium (mg):	583	meat:	5
		fat:	0

Turkey-Stuffed Peppers

6 medium green bell peppers
1 lb. ground turkey
1 cup cooked rice
2 tablespoons onion, minced
1 tablespoon Worchestershire sauce
1 clove garlic, minced
¼ teaspoon pepper
1 cup (8 oz.) light tomato sauce
½ cup water
¼ cup part-skim mozzarella cheese

Serves 6.

Cut off tops of green peppers; remove seeds and membrane.

Mix turkey with rice, onion, Worchestershire sauce, garlic, and pepper. Mix half of tomato sauce with turkey mixture, then spoon mixture into peppers; cover.

Place in microwave oven and cook 18 to 22 minutes, giving dish quarter-turn every 5 minutes. Add water and remaining tomato sauce. Sprinkle cheese over each pepper. Recover and return to microwave. Cook 1 to 2 minutes until cheese melts.

To Freeze: Place in microwave-safe casserole; label and freeze for up to 2 months.

To Serve: Thaw. Cover with microwave-safe plastic wrap, and cook on High 3 to 5 minutes.

Per Serving:		Diabetic Exchanges per Serving:	
calories:	243	milk:	0
protein (gm):	20.8	vegetable:	1½
fat (gm):	10.3	fruit:	0
cholesterol (mg):	56	bread:	½
sodium (mg):	420	meat:	2½
		fat:	½

12

FISH OUT OF WATER

AND

OTHER SEAFOOD

Filet of Sole Veracruzana

This is a favorite summer fish recipe because I make it with peppers, fresh tomatoes, chilies, and herbs from my garden.

1 tablespoon olive oil, divided
¼ cup onion, diced
1 garlic clove, minced
½ cup green bell pepper, diced
¼ cup chilies, diced
1 can (15½ oz.) chunky tomatoes
1 cup fresh tomato, cubed
2 tablespoons white wine
4 pitted black olives, sliced
10 ozs. sole filets
2 tablespoons fresh cilantro, chopped
2 tablespoons fresh parsley, chopped

Serves 2.

In a 1-quart casserole, place 1 teaspoon oil, onion, and garlic and cover. Microwave on High 2 minutes. Remove from oven and place remaining ingredients in casserole. Cover. Microwave on High 10 to 12 minutes, giving dish half-turn after 5 minutes. Remove from oven and let stand, covered, about 2 minutes before serving.

To Freeze: Label casserole and freeze for up to 2 months.

To Serve: Thaw. Cover with microwave-safe plastic wrap, and cook on High 3 to 5 minutes.

Per Serving:		Diabetic Exchanges per Serving:	
calories:	254	milk:	0
protein (gm):	29.4	vegetable:	1
fat (gm):	10.3	fruit:	0
cholesterol (mg):	76	bread:	0
sodium (mg):	345	meat:	3
		fat:	2

113

Cioppino

1 large onion, thinly sliced
1 cup scallions, chopped
3 cloves garlic, minced
½ cup fresh parsley, chopped
1 green bell pepper, seeded
  and diced
1 cup tomato, chopped
1 (14½-oz.) can no-salt-added
  chunky tomatoes
1 cup dry white wine
1 cup water
1 teaspoon thyme
1 teaspoon tarragon
¼ teaspoon rosemary
¼ teaspoon black pepper,
  freshly ground
1 bay leaf
1 lb. crabmeat, flaked; or firm
  white fish, cubed
1 lb. shrimp, shelled and
  deveined
16 scallops or clams, in shells
Serves 6.

Combine onion, scallions, and garlic in a large stockpot and cook, covered, over low heat till soft, stirring frequently. Add remaining ingredients, except seafood, and mix well. Continue to simmer, covered, for 1 hour. Add seafood and continue to cook, covered, for 8 to 10 minutes or until scallops are opaque or clams are open.

To Freeze: Vacuum seal each portion; label casserole and freeze for up to 2 months.

To Serve: Put bags in boiling water, and bring water to a boil again. Boil 10 to 12 minutes.

Per Serving:		Diabetic Exchanges per Serving:	
calories:	247	milk:	0
protein (gm):	37.3	vegetable:	1
fat (gm):	3.2	fruit:	0
cholesterol (mg):	236	bread:	0
sodium (mg):	641	meat:	4
		fat:	0

Poached Salmon

Poach a large piece of salmon—enough for two meals. Serve half of it warm in this recipe and the remainder in the next recipe, Marinated Salmon with Pasta.

2 lb. (or larger) piece of salmon

½ cup dry white wine
½ cup water
1 teaspoon celery salt
1 teaspoon Spike
2 green onions, sliced
1 tablespoon lemon juice
½ lemon, thinly sliced
Meal No. 1.
Serves 4.

Place salmon in crockpot. Pour in wine and water. Add celery salt, Spike, onions, and lemon juice. Place lemon slices across salmon. Cover and cook on Low 2 to 3 hours or until salmon flakes when tested with a fork.

Remove salmon from crockpot. Strain poaching juices into plastic container and refrigerate for soup. Remove skin and bones from salmon. Cut half of salmon into 4 serving-size pieces. Place on platter with 4 dollops of mustard on top of each piece.

To Freeze: Place in microwave-safe casserole; label and freeze for up to 2 months.

To Serve: Thaw. Cover with microwave-safe plastic wrap, and cook on High 3 to 5 minutes.

Per Serving:		Diabetic Exchanges per Serving:	
calories:	180	milk:	0
protein (gm):	25.0	vegetable:	0
fat (gm):	5.5	fruit:	0
cholesterol (mg):	44	bread:	0
sodium (mg):	75	meat:	3
		fat:	0

Marinated Salmon with Pasta

1 lb. cooked salmon (from previous recipe)
2 medium tomatoes, chopped (about 1½ cups)
1 onion, thinly sliced and separated into rings
½ cup pitted black olives, sliced
2 cloves garlic, crushed
2 tablespoons olive oil

2 tablespoons parsley, minced
½ teaspoon dried basil leaves
1 teaspoon dried oregano leaves
¼ teaspoon pepper, freshly ground
2 cups uncooked pasta bows
Lettuce leaves
¼ cup carrots, shredded (optional)
Meal No. 2.
Serves 4.

Mix all ingredients except pasta, lettuce, and carrots. Cover and refrigerate while you cook pasta. Cook pasta as directed on package; drain. Toss with salmon mixture. Refrigerate until ready to serve. Serve on lettuce and garnish with carrots.

To Freeze: Place individual portions of pasta and salmon mixture in separate vacuum-sealed bags; label and freeze for up to 2 months.

To Serve: Put bags in boiling water, and bring water to a boil again. Boil 10 to 12 minutes. Add garnishes such as parsley or cheese just before serving.

Per Serving:		Diabetic Exchanges per Serving:	
calories:	388	milk:	0
protein (gm):	35.4	vegetable:	0
fat (gm):	17.8	fruit:	0
cholesterol (mg):	75	bread:	1
sodium (mg):	127	meat:	4
		fat:	2

Salmon Cakes with Dill Sauce

1 lb. potatoes, peeled and quartered
1 can (15½ oz.) salmon
¼ cup low-fat yogurt
¼ cup green onions, sliced

3 tablespoons fresh parsley, chopped
2 tablespoons lemon juice
¼ teaspoon cracked pepper
1 cup fresh breadcrumbs
2 tablespoons olive oil
1 teaspoon diet margarine
1 recipe Dill Sauce (see p. 162)
Serves 6.

Place potatoes, with water to cover, in stockpot and cook until fork-tender, about 20 minutes. Drain and mash. Combine with potatoes remaining ingredients except olive oil, margarine, and Dill Sauce.

Mix well and shape into 6 large patties. Heat olive oil and margarine in stockpot and cook 3 patties until browned, about 5 minutes per side. Transfer to plate. Repeat with remaining patties. Serve with Dill Sauce.

To Freeze: Place in microwave-safe casserole; label and freeze for up to 2 months.

To Serve: Thaw. Cover with microwave-safe plastic wrap, and cook on High 3 to 5 minutes.

Per Serving:		Diabetic Exchanges per Serving:	
calories:	328	milk:	½
protein (gm):	22.0	vegetable:	0
fat (gm):	11.3	fruit:	0
cholesterol (mg):	5	bread:	2
sodium (mg):	587	meat:	2
		fat:	1

Scallops with Apples and Pea Pods

12 ozs. fresh or frozen scallops
¼ cup apple cider or juice
2 teaspoons cornstarch
1 tablespoon soy sauce
2 tablespoons cooking oil

3 small apples, cored and sliced
1 medium onion, chopped
1 medium red bell pepper, chopped
1 package (6 oz.) frozen pea pods or 1 cup fresh peas with pods

Serves 4.

Thaw scallops if frozen. Cut up any large scallops. Stir apple juice into cornstarch; stir in soy sauce. Set aside.

Heat wok over high heat; add 1 tablespoon oil. Stir-fry apples, onion, and pepper 3 minutes or until just tender; remove from wok.

Add remaining oil to wok. Stir-fry scallops 4 to 5 minutes or until done. Stir soy mixture and add it to scallops. Cook and stir till thickened and bubbly; cook and stir 2 minutes more. Stir pea pods into scallop mixture; stir in apples, onion, and pepper mixture. Cover and cook 1 to 2 minutes until pea pods are done.

To Freeze: Vacuum seal each portion; label and freeze for up to 2 months.

To Serve: Put bags in boiling water, and bring water to a boil again. Boil 10 to 12 minutes.

Per Serving:		Diabetic Exchanges per Serving:	
calories:	235	milk:	0
protein (gm):	18.7	vegetable:	½
fat (gm):	8.3	fruit:	1
cholesterol (mg):	37	bread:	0
sodium (mg):	449	meat:	2
		fat:	1½

Scallops with Mushrooms in Wine Sauce

I love to serve this dish in large seashells.

1 lb. scallops
1 cup dry white wine
2 tablespoons diet unsalted margarine
2 scallions, chopped
1 cup fresh mushrooms, sliced
5 tablespoons diet unsalted margarine
3 tablespoons flour
½ cup evaporated skim milk
¼ cup chives, snipped
1 cup soft breadcrumbs
Parsley for garnish

Serves 4.

Place scallops in bottom of casserole dish and add wine. Microwave, covered, 4 to 6 minutes on Medium-High until scallops are tender. Do not overcook. Strain and reserve liquid.

Place 2 tablespoons margarine in a 2-cup glass measure and add scallions and mushrooms. Microwave on High 3 to 5 minutes.

Wine Sauce:
In microwave on High, melt 3 tablespoons margarine in a 4-cup glass, about 45 to 50 seconds. Add reserved wine liquid and flour to margarine and whisk together. Microwave on High 2 minutes; add milk and chives, whisking well. Microwave on High 2 to 4 minutes more until thick enough to coat a spoon, whisking every 2 minutes.

Add scallions, mushrooms, and scallops to sauce and heat 2 minutes on Medium-High until hot.

Melt the remaining 2 tablespoons of margarine in a small bowl, on High 45 to 55 seconds, and add breadcrumbs until combined. Sprinkle over scallop mixture and garnish with parsley.

To Freeze: Vacuum seal each portion; label and freeze for up to 2 months.

To Serve: Put bags in boiling water, and bring water to a boil again. Boil 10 to 12 minutes.

Per Serving:		Diabetic Exchanges per Serving:	
calories:	371	milk:	½
protein (gm):	25.6	vegetable:	0
fat (gm):	12.2	fruit:	0
cholesterol (mg):	38	bread:	1
sodium (mg):	441	meat:	3
		fat:	2

Scallops in White Wine

¼ cup diet margarine
¼ cup dry white wine
3 tablespoons parsley, minced

1 tablespoon shallots or green onions, chopped
2 tablespoons light, dry sherry
1 teaspoon tarragon
1 teaspoon thyme
1 lb. scallops
½ lb. mushrooms, sliced
Serves 4.

Combine margarine, wine, parsley, shallots or onions, sherry, and herbs in crockpot. Cook, uncovered, on High until sauce bubbles and is reduced slightly. Add scallops and mushrooms. Cover. Cook 10 to 15 minutes or until cooked through.

To Freeze: Vacuum seal each portion; label and freeze for up to 2 months.

To Serve: Put bags in boiling water, and bring water to a boil again. Boil 10 to 12 minutes.

Per Serving:		Diabetic Exchanges per Serving:	
calories:	186	milk:	0
protein (gm):	20.3	vegetable:	1
fat (gm):	6.8	fruit:	0
cholesterol (mg):	37	bread:	0
sodium (mg):	325	meat:	2
		fat:	1

Shrimp Diane

1 lb. medium shrimps, shelled and deveined
1 lemon, sliced
¼ cup white wine
1 tablespoon margarine
2 tablespoons shallots, finely minced

½ cup mushrooms, thinly sliced
8 artichoke hearts
¼ cup chives, snipped
4 tablespoons chopped pimiento
Parsley sprigs for garnish
Serves 4.

Prepare sauce first by combining wine, margarine, and shallots in a saucepan. Place over medium-high heat, cover, and bring to boil. Lower heat and add mushrooms, artichoke hearts, chives, and pimiento. Simmer 2 minutes. Keep warm.

Use a steamer large enough so shrimp can be steamed directly on rack in a single layer. Steam over water to which 1 sliced lemon has been added. Steam shrimp about 2 minutes or until they turn pink. Watch carefully, as to not overcook.

Once shrimp are steamed, add to saucepan containing wine sauce. With two spoons, mix shrimp with sauce and remove from heat. Spoon shrimp over rice or couscous.

To Freeze: Vacuum seal each portion; label and freeze for up to 2 months.

To Serve: Put bags in boiling water, and bring water to a boil again. Boil 10 to 12 minutes.

Per Serving:		Diabetic Exchanges per Serving:	
calories:	198	milk:	0
protein (gm):	26.9	vegetable:	2
fat (gm):	3.0	fruit:	0
cholesterol (mg):	221	bread:	0
sodium (mg):	374	meat:	3
		fat:	0

Peking Shrimp

6 dried black mushrooms
4 green onions (with tops)
16 pea pods (fresh, preferred, or frozen)
¾ lb. raw medium shrimp (in shells)
1 teaspoon arrowroot
1 teaspoon water
2 tablespoons vegetable oil
2 teaspoons garlic, finely chopped
¼ cup Chicken Stock (see page 36)
Serves 4.

Soak mushrooms in hot water 20 minutes or until soft; drain. Squeeze out excess moisture. Remove and discard stems; cut caps into thin strips.

Cut green onions diagonally into 1-in. pieces. Cut pea pods into 1-in. pieces. Peel shrimp, wash, and devein. Pat dry with paper towels. Mix arrowroot and water.

Heat wok until very hot. Add 2 tablespoons vegetable oil; tilt wok to coat side. Add shrimp and garlic; stir-fry until shrimp are pink. Remove shrimp from wok.

Add mushrooms, green onions, and pea pods to wok and stir-fry 2 minutes. Add Chicken Stock and bring to boil. Cover and cook 1 minute. Stir in arrowroot mixture and return shrimp to wok. Cook and stir 30 seconds or until shrimp are hot.

To Freeze: Vacuum seal each portion; label and freeze for up to 2 months.

To Serve: Put bags in boiling water, and bring water to a boil again. Boil 10 to 12 minutes.

Per Serving:		Diabetic Exchanges per Serving:	
calories:	146	milk:	0
protein (gm):	15.9	vegetable:	0
fat (gm):	7.7	fruit:	0
cholesterol (mg):	138	bread:	0
sodium (mg):	208	meat:	2
		fat:	1

Poached Shrimp

I prefer this basic procedure to boiling.

8 cups water
¼ cup onion, sliced

1 clove garlic
1 bay leaf
2 celery ribs with leaves
2 lbs. shrimp
½ lemon, sliced
Serves 4.

Combine ingredients in stockpot. Wash, drain, and add shrimp; add lemon. Simmer shrimp about 5 minutes or until pink but not tightly curled. Drain immediately and chill.

Before serving, remove shells, but leave tails intact.

To Freeze: Vacuum seal each portion; label and freeze for up to 2 months.

To Serve: Put bags in boiling water, and bring water to a boil again. Boil 10 to 12 minutes.

Per Serving:		Diabetic Exchanges per Serving:	
calories:	179	milk:	0
protein (gm):	37.9	vegetable:	0
fat (gm):	1.9	fruit:	0
cholesterol (mg):	354	bread:	0
sodium (mg):	406	meat:	4
		fat:	0

13
A PIECE OF CAKE

Today, with everyone working and leading such busy lives, baking has almost become a thing of the past. Yet baking has become easier than ever thanks to miraculous mixes you can use in a conventional oven or microwave. You can even make a cake in a crockpot while you're off at a meeting or shopping. Best of all, when dieting, dessert and especially cake can become low calorie if you make it yourself.

In this chapter you will find a recipe for a Basic Chocolate Baking Mix that will allow you to make cupcakes, brownies, and cake from the same recipe. If you keep a batch of this mix in your pantry, you will be prepared for anything. You should also consider stocking frozen dough, frozen puff pastry, and frozen phyllo dough because each lends itself to quick and delicious treats.

If you keep several pre-baked cakes in your freezer, such as chocolate sponge cake or layer cake, you can prepare a filling or frosting in just minutes. The result will be a dessert equal to any you may have spent all day baking.

Baking Tips

• Be sure to read the recipe through twice before starting to bake.

• Assemble all ingredients before beginning recipe.

• If using a crockpot to bake, remember that a 1- or 2-lb. coffee can makes a good baker if you do not have a crockpot bake pan.

• In a crockpot, be sure to cover your cake mold to keep out condensed steam. I like to use a Pyrex cover on a mold. Prop it slightly with a twist

124

of foil so steam can escape. The glass cover is nice because you can see what is happening to your cake.

• A Bread'n Cake bake pan has been designed for use in the crockpot.

• The larger 5½-qt. crockpot is best to use for baking, but the 3½-qt. can be used to make smaller cakes.

Important News for Chocolate Lovers

Unsweetened cocoa is the only chocolate baking ingredient approved by the American Heart Association for use in fat-restricted diets. To make a delicious and healthier version of your favorite chocolate dessert, follow these easy substitution tips:

• For every 1-oz. square of unsweetened baking chocolate, you can substitute 3 level tablespoons of cocoa plus 1 tablespoon of shortening (liquid or solid).

• For each 1-oz. envelope of pre-melted unsweetened chocolate, you can substitute 3 tablespoons of cocoa plus 1 tablespoon of oil or melted shortening.

Yogurt Cheesecake

2 cups unflavored Yogurt
  Cheese (see p. 147)
Vegetable spray, non-stick

½ cup graham cracker crumbs
¼ cup sugar
1 tablespoon cornstarch
6 egg whites
1 tablespoon vanilla
Serves 8.

Make Yogurt Cheese recipe, omitting seasonings and draining for 24 hours.

Heat oven to 325°.

For crust, spray a 7-in. spring-form pan with non-stick vegetable spray. Sprinkle with graham cracker crumbs. Refrigerate crust while making filling.

Beat Yogurt Cheese, sugar, and cornstarch in medium-size mixer bowl until creamy. Beat in egg whites and vanilla. Pour into prepared 7-in. pan. Bake until set, 45 to 55 minutes. Turn off oven and let cake remain in oven 1 hour. Remove cake from oven and refrigerate.

Note: You can serve with sauce, such as chocolate or raspberry, or with plain fresh fruit to taste. Another idea is to sprinkle a mixture of sugar or Equal® with cinnamon over the top.

Note: It is not recommended that you freeze this cake.

Per Serving:		Diabetic Exchanges per Serving:	
calories:	156	milk:	1
protein (gm):	8.5	vegetable:	0
fat (gm):	3.8	fruit:	0
cholesterol (mg):	6	bread:	½
sodium (mg):	173	meat:	0
		fat:	1

Apple Cake

I love this cake because everything goes into one bowl, which makes it fast to make. And it packs well for lunches or picnics.

Vegetable spray, non-stick
⅔ cup sugar
½ cup packed brown sugar
¼ cup vegetable oil
3 egg whites
⅔ cup cake flour (all-purpose flour may be used, if preferred)
⅔ cup whole-wheat flour
½ cup bran cereal (bran buds, etc.)
1½ teaspoons baking soda
1 teaspoon ground cinnamon
¼ teaspoon ground allspice
3 cups apples, unpeeled and shredded
½ cup low-fat yogurt
Powdered sugar (optional)

Serves 16.

Spray a 13×9×2-in. baking pan with non-stick vegetable spray.

In a large bowl, combine sugars, oil, and egg whites. Beat with a wooden spoon till well blended. Add flours, cereal, baking soda, cinnamon, and allspice; stir just till moistened. Stir in the yogurt and shredded apples. Pour batter into prepared pan.

Bake in 350° oven 25 to 30 minutes. Cool. Sift powdered sugar onto cake.

To Freeze: Wrap cake in aluminum foil; label and freeze for up to 2 months.

To Serve: Thaw and slice to serve.

Per Serving:		Diabetic Exchanges per Serving:	
calories:	149	milk:	0
protein (gm):	2.5	vegetable:	0
fat (gm):	3.8	fruit:	0
cholesterol (mg):	0	bread:	1½
sodium (mg):	111	meat:	0
		fat:	1

Light Pound Cake

I always have several of these in the freezer. You can serve this cake with a sauce, yogurt, or fresh fruit.

2¼ cups unbleached all-purpose flour
¾ teaspoon baking powder
¼ teaspoon baking soda
¼ teaspoon salt
½ cup (1 stick) corn-oil margarine, softened
1 cup sugar
3 egg whites
1½ teaspoons vanilla extract
¾ cup buttermilk
Vegetable spray, non-stick
Serves 16.

Heat oven to 350°.

Put flour, baking powder, baking soda, and salt into medium bowl. Mix well and set aside.

Cream margarine and sugar in large bowl until smooth. Beat in egg whites and vanilla until smooth. Alternately add flour mixture and buttermilk in two batches each, blending well after each addition.

Spoon batter into a 7 × 4½-in. loaf pan that has been sprayed with non-stick vegetable spray. Bake until golden and cake has pulled away from sides of pan, about 1 hour. Cool on wire rack.

Lemon Pound Cake
Substitute 2 teaspoons lemon juice for vanilla extract, and add the grated zest of 1 lemon.

To Freeze: Wrap cake in aluminum foil; label and freeze for up to 2 months.

To Serve: Thaw and slice to serve.

Per Serving:		Diabetic Exchanges per Serving:	
calories:	164	milk:	0
protein (gm):	2.7	vegetable:	0
fat (gm):	5.9	fruit:	0
cholesterol (mg):	0	bread:	2
sodium (mg):	151	meat:	0
		fat:	1

Chocolate Sponge Cake

I keep several of these cakes in the freezer for unexpected guests. This cake can be dressed as a roll, torte, or filled with pudding or fruit. It will please your most discriminating guest.

5 egg whites

⅛ teaspoon salt
⅛ teaspoon cream of tartar
½ cup granulated sugar
½ cup sifted cake flour
½ cup cocoa
2 teaspoons strong coffee
½ teaspoon vanilla
¼ teaspoon chocolate extract
3 tablespoons confectioner's sugar
Serves 10.

Line a 15 × 10-in. jelly-roll pan with greased wax paper.

In large bowl, beat egg whites, salt, and cream of tartar until mixture just mounds on spoon (not quite to soft peak stage). Using spatula, fold in granulated sugar, a large spoonful at a time. Sift half the flour over egg white mixture and fold gently; repeat with remaining flour. Add cocoa and mix well. Fold in coffee, vanilla, and chocolate extract.

Spread in prepared pan and bake in 300° oven 25 minutes or until firm to touch. Sift half the confectioner's sugar over cake; cover with tea towel and invert baking pan. Carefully remove wax paper, using sharp knife. Trim any crusty edges.

While cake is hot, roll up in towel, jelly-roll fashion; let cool. Make filling if using cake as jelly roll. Cake and filling can be prepared to this point, covered, and refrigerated up to 1 day.

Unroll cake and spread evenly with filling. Roll up, using towel to help roll. Sift remaining confectioner's sugar over top. Place seam-side-down on serving platter.

For Torte

Gently transfer unrolled Chocolate Sponge Cake to wire rack; cover and cool completely. Cut into 3 (10 × 5-in.) rectangles.

Spread White Chocolate or Strawberry Mousse (see Index) filling evenly over each rectangle and stack rectangles, filling-side-up, on platter; cover and chill 1 hour. Cut stack in half lengthwise; place cake halves side by side on serving platter, cut-side-down. Cover and chill 30 minutes. Spoon sauce on top.

To Freeze: Wrap cake in aluminum foil; label and freeze for up to 2 months.

To Serve: Thaw and slice to serve.

Per Serving:		Diabetic Exchanges per Serving:	
calories:	83	milk:	0
protein (gm):	3.3	vegetable:	0
fat (gm):	0.7	fruit:	0
cholesterol (mg):	0	bread:	1
sodium (mg):	57	meat:	½
		fat:	0

Quick Chocolate Cake

1 cup all-purpose flour
½ cup whole-wheat flour
1 teaspoon baking powder
½ teaspoon baking soda
¾ cup sugar
3 tablespoons unsweetened cocoa
1 teaspoon ground cinnamon
1 cup water
2 tablespoons vegetable oil
2 teaspoons mocha extract
1 teaspoon vinegar
2 egg whites, beaten

Serves 16.

Combine first 7 ingredients in 8-in.-square baking pan; make well in center of mixture. Combine water and rest of ingredients; add to dry ingredients. Stir until well blended. Bake at 350° 30 minutes or until wooden pick inserted in center comes out clean. Cool in pan on wire rack.

To Freeze: Wrap cake in aluminum foil; label and freeze for up to 2 months.

To Serve: Defrost on countertop and serve.

Per Serving:		Diabetic Exchanges per Serving:	
calories:	94	milk:	0
protein (gm):	1.9	vegetable:	0
fat (gm):	1.9	fruit:	0
cholesterol (mg):	0	bread:	1
sodium (mg):	18	meat:	0
		fat:	½

Mocha Minute Frosting

3 tablespoons cocoa
1 cup granulated sugar

⅓ cup evaporated skim milk
¼ cup diet margarine
1 teaspoon instant coffee
   granules
1 teaspoon mocha extract
Serves 20.

Mix all ingredients except mocha extract. Bring to boil and simmer 1 minute. Remove from heat, add mocha extract, and beat until thick enough to spread.

To Freeze: Place in freezer container; label and freeze for up to 2 months.

To Serve: Thaw, then use as desired.

Per Serving:		Diabetic Exchanges per Serving:	
calories:	50	milk:	0
protein (gm):	0.3	vegetable:	0
fat (gm):	1.2	fruit:	0
cholesterol (mg):	0	bread:	½
sodium (mg):	28	meat:	0
		fat:	½

Basic Chocolate Baking Mix

This basic mix is a favorite be-cause you can make a dessert on a moment's notice. Cup-cakes, brownies, or a cake (recipes follow) can be made from the same mix, which you keep on your pantry shelf. What could be faster!

3 cups sugar
2 cups unsifted all-purpose flour
2 cups unsweetened cocoa powder
1½ teaspoons baking powder
Makes 7 cups.
Serves 7.

Combine all ingredients in zip-close bag. Shake thoroughly to mix. Store in bag or canister with tight-fitting lid.

To Store: Place in air-tight container; such as Tupperware, and store for up to 1 year.

Per Serving:		Diabetic Exchanges per Serving:	
calories:	499	milk:	0
protein (gm):	10.0	vegetable:	0
fat (gm):	4.0	fruit:	0
cholesterol (mg):	0	bread:	7
sodium (mg):	90	meat:	0
		fat:	0

Chocolate Cake

2 cups Basic Chocolate Baking Mix (recipe p. 133)

Egg substitute equalling 2 eggs
½ cup light mayonnaise
½ cup skim milk
Serves 12.

Mix all ingredients in bowl. Pour into greased 9-in. round cake pan. Preheat oven to 350° and bake 25 minutes.

Note: Check Sauce chapter for a delicious topping for your cake. Or frost with Mocha Minute Frosting (recipe p. 132).

To Freeze: Wrap in aluminum foil; label and freeze for up to 2 months.

To Serve: Defrost cake and serve.

Per Serving:		Diabetic Exchanges per Serving:	
calories:	190	milk:	0
protein (gm):	3.8	vegetable:	0
fat (gm):	8.5	fruit:	0
cholesterol (mg):	3	bread:	1½
sodium (mg):	55	meat:	0
		fat:	2

Football Cake

1 Chocolate Cake (above recipe)
1 recipe Mocha Minute Frosting (see p. 132)
Serves 6.

When cool, cut a 2-in. slice from center of cake; rejoin halves to create oval shape. Spread chocolate frosting on sides and top of cake. Using frosting tube, make laces on football. Garnish by placing shredded coconut and gumdrops around cake.

Cupcakes

1 cup Basic Chocolate Baking
Mix (recipe p. 133)
2 egg whites

¼ cup light mayonnaise
¼ cup skim milk
Serves 6.

Mix all ingredients in bowl. Preheat oven to 350° and bake 18 to 20 minutes in paper-lined, 6-muffin pan.

To Freeze: Wrap cupcakes in aluminum foil and label. Freeze for up to 2 months.

To Serve: Thaw and serve.

Per Serving:		Diabetic Exchanges per Serving:	
calories:	119	milk:	0
protein (gm):	3.2	vegetable:	0
fat (gm):	3.3	fruit:	0
cholesterol (mg):	3	bread:	1
sodium (mg):	38	meat:	0
		fat:	1

Brownies

2 cups Basic Chocolate Baking
   Mix (recipe p. 133)

Egg substitute equalling 2 eggs
½ cup light mayonnaise
¼ cup skim milk
Serves 20.

Mix all ingredients in bowl. Spread on 9×9-in. baking pan. Pre-heat oven to 350° and bake 20 to 25 minutes.

To Freeze: Cut brownies into squares, Wrap in aluminum foil and label. Freeze for up to 2 months.

To Serve: Thaw and serve.

Per Serving:		Diabetic Exchanges per Serving:	
calories:	72	milk:	0
protein (gm):	1.8	vegetable:	0
fat (gm):	2.2	fruit:	0
cholesterol (mg):	2	bread:	½
sodium (mg):	21	meat:	0
		fat:	½

Chocolate Hearts with Assorted Berries

1 Chocolate Sponge Cake (see recipe, p. 129)
1 cup powdered sugar

½ cup strawberries, sliced
½ cup raspberries
½ cup blackberries
2 teaspoons sugar
1 recipe Chocolate Sauce (see recipes, pp. 155–57)

Serves 14.

Cut cake into 28 hearts, using 2½-in. heart-shaped cookie cutter; discard remaining cake. Sprinkle cake hearts with powdered sugar; set aside.

Combine berries with sugar and mix well.

To serve, spoon about 1 tablespoon Chocolate Sauce onto plate; top with cake heart, 2 tablespoons berries, and another cake heart. Repeat procedure with remaining ingredients.

To Freeze: Freeze chocolate hearts by wrapping them in aluminum foil, labeling, and freezing for up to 2 months. Freeze berries by placing them in a vacuum-sealed bag and freezing for up to 2 months.

To Serve: Thaw and serve.

Per Serving:		**Diabetic Exchanges per Serving:**	
calories:	77	milk:	0
protein (gm):	2.6	vegetable:	0
fat (gm):	0.6	fruit:	0
cholesterol (mg):	0	bread:	1
sodium (mg):	41	meat:	0
		fat:	0

Gingerbread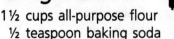

1½ cups all-purpose flour
½ teaspoon baking soda
1 teaspoon cinnamon
1 teaspoon ginger
½ teaspoon cloves
⅛ teaspoon nutmeg

¼ cup diet margarine
½ cup sugar
2 egg whites
½ cup light molasses
2 tablespoons hot water
½ cup buttermilk

Serves 8.

Mix flour with baking soda and spices; set aside.

Cream margarine with sugar. Add egg whites and beat well. Combine molasses and hot water; add gradually to creamed mixture, blending well. Alternately, add dry ingredients in thirds and buttermilk in halves to creamed mixture, beating until smooth after each addition.

Turn into well-greased and floured 2-lb. coffee can. Cover and place in crockpot. Cook on High 2 to 3 hours.

Note: Low-calorie whipped topping is nice on top of gingerbread.

To Freeze: Vacuum seal individual portions; label and freeze for up to 2 months.

To Serve: Put bags in boiling water, and bring to a boil again. Boil 10 to 12 minutes.

*Per Serving:		Diabetic Exchanges per Serving:	
calories:	209	milk:	0
protein (gm):	3.6	vegetable:	0
fat (gm):	3.1	fruit:	0
cholesterol (mg):	0	bread:	2½
sodium (mg):	150	meat:	0
		fat:	½

*Without whipped topping.

14

SWEET TOOTH TREATS

Important News for Chocolate Lovers

Unsweetened cocoa is the only chocolate baking ingredient approved by the American Heart Association for use in fat-restricted diets. To make a delicious and healthier version of your favorite chocolate dessert, follow these easy substitution tips:

• For every 1-oz. square of unsweetened baking chocolate, you can substitute 3 level tablespoons of cocoa plus 1 tablespoon of shortening (liquid or solid).

• For each 1-oz. envelope of pre-melted unsweetened chocolate, you can substitute 3 tablespoons of cocoa plus 1 tablespoon of oil or melted shortening.

Strawberry Mousse or Filling

1 envelope unflavored gelatin
¼ cup orange juice
3 cups fresh strawberries
¼ cup confectioner's sugar

1 envelope low-calorie
    whipped topping
4 egg whites
¼ cup granulated sugar
Fresh berries, hulled (to garnish mousse)
Serves 6.

In small microwave-safe dish, sprinkle gelatin over orange juice and let stand 5 minutes to soften. Microwave on High 10 seconds until gelatin has dissolved.

Hull strawberries and place in blender; add confectioner's sugar and process until smooth. Transfer to mixing bowl and stir in gelatin mixture. Refrigerate until mixture has consistency of raw egg whites (about 20 minutes).

Whip low-calorie topping and set aside.

In large bowl, beat egg whites until soft peaks form; gradually add granulated sugar, beating until stiff peaks form. Whisk about ¼ of the beaten egg whites into strawberry mixture. Fold straw-berry mixture along with whipped topping into remaining egg whites.

Pour into 6-cup serving bowl or individual dessert dishes. You can also use this mousse as a filling for Chocolate Sponge Cake (see Index).

To Freeze: Place in freezer container, label, and freeze for up to 2 months.

To Serve: Thaw, then use as you like.

Per Serving:		Diabetic Exchanges per Serving:	
calories:	114	milk:	0
protein (gm):	4.3	vegetable:	0
fat (gm):	1.9	fruit:	½
cholesterol (mg):	1	bread:	1
sodium (mg):	48	meat:	0
		fat:	½

Strawberry Tulips

12 large strawberries
3 ozs. Yogurt Cheese (see
  page 147), softened
2 tablespoons powdered sugar

1 tablespoon light sour cream
1 tablespoon orange rind,
  grated
Mint leaves for garnish
(optional)
Serves 6.

Remove stems from berries, forming a flat base. Place berries pointed end up. Using a sharp knife, carefully slice berries in half vertically through the center to within ¼ in. of base. Cut each half into 3 wedges, forming 6 petals (do not slice through base). Pull petals apart gently.

In small bowl, beat Yogurt Cheese, powdered sugar, sour cream, and orange rind until light and fluffy. Using a small spoon, fill berries with yogurt mixture. Garnish with mint in place of stems if desired. (This is a delightful mini-dessert to serve with coffee after a large meal.)

To Freeze: Place in microwave-safe container; label, and freeze for up to 2 months.

To Serve: Thaw in refrigerator and garnish before serving if desired.

Per Serving:		Diabetic Exchanges per Serving:	
calories:	111	milk:	0
protein (gm):	2.1	vegetable:	0
fat (gm):	8.7	fruit:	1
cholesterol (mg):	17	bread:	0
sodium (mg):	33	meat:	0
		fat:	2

White Chocolate Mousse or Filling

1½ tablespoons unflavored
   gelatin
½ cup skim milk
6 ozs. white chocolate

1 teaspoon vanilla
1 cup low-calorie whipped
   topping
¼ teaspoon lemon juice
2 egg whites
Chocolate curls, shaved
(optional)
Serves 6.

Soften gelatin in milk. When gelatin is dissolved, transfer to top of double boiler. Add chocolate. Stir over simmering water until melted. Remove from heat. Stir in vanilla. Transfer to large bowl and cool.

Beat low-calorie topping. Carefully fold into chocolate mixture. Add lemon juice to egg whites. Beat until stiff peaks form. Carefully fold into chocolate mixture. Spoon into 6 glass dessert dishes and chill, or use as filling for Chocolate Sponge Cake (see p. 129).

To Freeze: Place in microwave-safe casserole; label and freeze for up to 2 months.

To Serve: Thaw in refrigerator and garnish before serving.

Per Serving:		Diabetic Exchanges per Serving:	
calories:	191	milk:	0
protein (gm):	5.3	vegetable:	0
fat (gm):	10.8	fruit:	0
cholesterol (mg):	1	bread:	1
sodium (mg):	67	meat:	½
		fat:	2

Chocolate Rum Balls

3½ cups (about 12 ozs.) vanilla wafer crumbs

1 cup confectioner's sugar, divided
¼ cup unsweetened cocoa
⅓ cup dark or light rum
⅓ cup light or dark corn syrup

Makes about 4 dozen.
Serves 24: 2 per serving.

Combine ingredients, using only ½ cup confectioner's sugar, in bowl and mix well. Shape into 1-in. balls. Roll in reserved ½ cup confectioner's sugar. Store in tightly covered container.

Chocolate Bourbon Balls: Follow basic recipe above but substitute ⅓ cup bourbon for rum.

To Freeze: Vacuum seal individual portions; label and freeze for up to 2 months.

To Serve: Thaw on counter or in refrigerator.

Per Serving:		Diabetic Exchanges per Serving:	
calories:	104	milk:	0
protein (gm):	0.9	vegetable:	0
fat (gm):	2.2	fruit:	0
cholesterol (mg):	8	bread:	1
sodium (mg):	39	meat:	0
		fat:	½

Chocolate Pudding

A good recipe hot or cold.

Margarine
8 tablespoons sugar, divided
8 ozs. semisweet chocolate
2 tablespoons fruit-only apricot
   jam

8 egg whites, divided
1 tablespoon breadcrumbs,
   finely ground
Salt, 1 pinch
¼ cup liqueur (Amaretto,
   brandy, rum, etc.) (optional)
Raspberry Sauce (see p. 158)
Mint, fresh for garnish
Serves 6.

Use margarine to grease a 1-qt. pudding mold, including inside of lid. Add about 3 tablespoons sugar, replace lid, and shake vigorously so entire surface is coated. Shake out any excess sugar. Set aside.

Melt chocolate over hot water. Stir. When melted, remove from heat and allow to cool slightly.

Put jam and 2 egg whites in large bowl and beat until well blended. Add 4 tablespoons sugar and beat until well mixed. Add breadcrumbs, liqueur, and melted chocolate. Mix well.

Beat remaining 6 egg whites with salt. When soft peaks have formed, add remaining tablespoon of sugar and continue beating until stiff.

Beat 4 tablespoons of egg whites into chocolate mixture and fold remainder in gently. Pour into prepared mold, cover, and steam 1 hour. If pudding is to be served hot, leave mold in steamer, with heat turned off, until serving time. If it is to be served cold, remove from steamer, cool, and refrigerate. Do not remove pudding from mold until ready to serve. When ready to serve, run knife around edges of pudding and unmold onto platter. Serve with Raspberry Sauce and mint garnish.

Note: It is not recommended that you freeze this dish.

Per Serving:		Diabetic Exchanges per Serving:	
calories:	326	milk:	0
protein (gm):	6.3	vegetable:	0
fat (gm):	15.5	fruit:	0
cholesterol (mg):	0	bread:	1½
sodium (mg):	175	meat:	1
		fat:	3½

No-Egg Rice Pudding

1 cup converted rice
2½ cups skim milk
⅔ cup sugar

½ cup golden raisins
½ teaspoon nutmeg
Peel of ½ lemon, grated
½ teaspoon vanilla extract
1½ cups low-calorie whipped topping

Serves 8.

Place all ingredients except whipped topping in crockpot and mix well. Cover and cook on Low 4 to 6 hours. Serve warm with whipped topping.

To Freeze: Vacuum seal each portion; label and freeze for up to 2 months.

To Serve: Put bags in boiling water, and bring water to a boil again. Boil 10 to 12 minutes.

Per Serving:		Diabetic Exchanges per Serving:	
calories:	228	milk:	½
protein (gm):	5.0	vegetable:	0
fat (gm):	2.1	fruit:	½
cholesterol (mg):	2	bread:	2
sodium (mg):	51	meat:	0
		fat:	½

Flan

¼ cup sugar
1 can (12 oz.) evaporated skim
   milk
½ cup skim milk
¾ cup egg substitute
¼ cup sugar

⅛ teaspoon salt
½ teaspoon almond extract
2 cups assorted fresh berries
   (strawberries, blueberries,
   raspberries)

Serves 6.

Sprinkle ¼ cup sugar into heavy saucepan; place over medium heat. Cook, stirring constantly, until sugar melts and syrup is golden brown. Pour into 6 (6-oz.) custard cups; let cool.

Combine milks in medium-size saucepan, and heat until bubbles form around edge of pan.

Combine egg substitute, ¼ cup sugar, salt, and almond extract; beat well. Gradually stir about 1 cup hot milk into egg mixture; add remaining milk, stirring constantly.

Pour mixture evenly into custard cups; cover with aluminum foil. Place custard cups in shallow pan; add hot water to depth of 1 in. Bake at 325° 25 minutes or until knife inserted near center comes out clean. Remove cups from water and chill at least 4 hours.

To serve, loosen edges of custard with spatula; invert onto plates. Arrange assorted berries around flan.

To Freeze: Place in microwave-safe casserole; label and freeze for up to 2 months.

To Serve: Thaw in refrigerator and garnish before serving if desired.

Per Serving:		Diabetic Exchanges per Serving:	
calories:	160	milk:	½
protein (gm):	9.0	vegetable:	0
fat (gm):	1.3	fruit:	½
cholesterol (mg):	2	bread:	1
sodium (mg):	178	meat:	½
		fat:	0

Mock Cream Cheese (Yogurt Cheese)

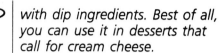

I think this is the greatest. You can serve it plain or dress it up with dip ingredients. Best of all, you can use it in desserts that call for cream cheese.

16 ozs. plain, non-fat yogurt

Makes about ¾ cup.
Serves 16.

Line strainer with double layer of cheesecloth or a large coffee filter. Pour in yogurt. Place yogurt-filled strainer over bowl, at least 1 in. above its bottom; refrigerate overnight. Scoop thickened yogurt into another bowl; discard cheesecloth. Use Mock Cream Cheese instead of mayonnaise or cream cheese on bread or as a base for dips.

To Freeze: Place in microwave-safe casserole; label and freeze for up to 2 months.

To Serve: Thaw in refrigerator and garnish before serving if desired.

Per Serving:		Diabetic Exchanges per Serving:	
calories:	29	milk:	½
protein (gm):	2.7	vegetable:	0
fat (gm):	0.8	fruit:	0
cholesterol (mg):	3	bread:	0
sodium (mg):	25	meat:	0
		fat:	0

15

FANCIFUL FRUIT

Autumn Fruit Compote

2 8-oz. packages mixed dried
  fruits
1 cup raisins
2½ cups apple cider

½ cup sugar or 12 packets
  Equal®
2 lemon slices
10 whole cloves
6-in. stick cinnamon
½ cup brandy
Whipped topping, non-fat
  (optional)
Serves 10.

Cut dried fruits into large pieces. In wok, place mixed dried fruits and raisins. Stir in apple cider and sugar. (If using Equal®, do not add until cooking is complete.) Bring to boil. Stud lemon slices with cloves; add to wok. Add stick cinnamon. Reduce heat; cover and simmer about 20 minutes or until fruit is tender. Discard lemon slices and stick cinnamon. Add brandy. Cool slightly. Spoon into serving dishes; top with non-fat whipped topping, if desired.

To Freeze: Vacuum seal each portion; label and freeze for up to 2 months.

To Serve: Put bags in boiling water, and bring water to a boil again. Boil 10 to 12 minutes.

Per Serving:		Diabetic Exchanges per Serving:	
calories:	184	milk:	0
protein (gm):	1.1	vegetable:	0
fat (gm):	0.2	fruit:	2
cholesterol (mg):	0	bread:	½
sodium (mg):	6	meat:	0
		fat:	1

Fresh Fruit Salad with Grand Marnier

This dessert is welcome any time of the year and can be made with any seasonal fruits.

Juice of 1 lemon
¼ cup sugar

3 tablespoons Grand Marnier
2 tablespoons honey
1 cup seedless orange sections
1 cup seedless green grapes
1 cup strawberries, hulled
1 cup blueberries
1 cup cantaloupe balls
1 cup raspberries
Serves 8.

Combine lemon juice, sugar, Grand Marnier, and honey. Add fruit and blend well. Chill until ready to serve. This fruit salad goes well with Chocolate Rum Balls (see Index).

To Freeze: Vacuum seal each portion; label and freeze for up to 2 months.

To Serve: Thaw in refrigerator or in bowl of water. Serve chilled.

Per Serving:		**Diabetic Exchanges per Serving:**	
calories:	107	milk:	0
protein (gm):	0.8	vegetable:	0
fat (gm):	0.3	fruit:	1
cholesterol (mg):	0	bread:	½
sodium (mg):	3	meat:	0
		fat:	0

Peaches Amaretto

8 cups fresh peaches (about 3
lbs.), peeled, sliced
Fruit Fresh (in canned goods
section of market)

½ cup amaretto
8 small amaretto cookies,
crushed, or 8 tablespoons
granola
Serves 8.

Combine peaches, Fruit Fresh, and amaretto in large dish; cover
and chill about 2 hours. Spoon into 8 dessert dishes; sprinkle with
cookies or granola.

To Freeze: Vacuum seal each portion; label and freeze for up to
2 months.

To Serve: Thaw in refrigerator or in bowl of water. Serve chilled.

Per Serving:		Diabetic Exchanges per Serving:	
calories:	196	milk:	0
protein (gm):	1.8	vegetable:	0
fat (gm):	3.7	fruit:	2
cholesterol (mg):	0	bread:	½
sodium (mg):	83	meat:	0
		fat:	1

Pears with Rum Raisin Sauce

4 ripe Bartlett pears (Bosc or Anjou can also be used)

Lemon juice, fresh
6 tablespoons Grand Marnier
Rum Raisin Sauce (see p. 159)
Serves 4.

Peel and core pears, rubbing each with lemon juice. Stand pears upright in shallow dish and pour 1½ tablespoons Grand Marnier over each pear. Set dish on rack over boiling water, cover pot, and steam 5 minutes. Baste pears with liquid in dish, and steam another 5 minutes.

Test pears to see if they are done by inserting a cake tester into one of them; the tester should go in easily, but the flesh of the pear should remain slightly firm. Baste again and steam an additional 2 minutes.

Transfer pears to individual serving plates and spoon Rum Raisin Sauce over each. Serve warm.

To Freeze: Vacuum seal each portion; label and freeze for up to 2 months.

To Serve: Put bags in boiling water, and bring water to a boil again. Boil 10 to 12 minutes.

Per Serving:		Diabetic Exchanges per Serving:	
calories:	252	milk:	½
protein (gm):	4.5	vegetable:	0
fat (gm):	0.7	fruit:	2
cholesterol (mg):	1	bread:	½
sodium (mg):	57	meat:	0
		fat:	1

Strawberry Rhubarb Compote

3 cups strawberries, hulled and sliced
¼ cup sugar
1 tablespoon fresh lemon juice

Cold water
2 tablespoons cornstarch
1 cup rhubarb, diced
½ teaspoon orange peel, grated
Yogurt, plain, non-fat
Orange slices (for garnish)
Serves 4.

Place first 3 ingredients in a bowl; mix well.

Dissolve cornstarch in water and add, with rhubarb and orange peel, to a small saucepan. Cook over medium heat until mixture boils and thickens and rhubarb is tender, stirring constantly, about 10 minutes. Transfer rhubarb mixture to bowl with strawberries and mix well.

Place entire fruit mixture in saucepan and heat on medium for about 10 minutes. Remove from heat and cool. Spoon into 4 wine goblets and refrigerate until well chilled, about 1 hour. Top compote with a dollop of yogurt and an orange slice.

To Freeze: Vacuum seal each portion; label and freeze for up to 2 months.

To Serve: Thaw in refrigerator or in bowl of water. Serve chilled.

Per Serving:		Diabetic Exchanges per Serving:	
calories:	115	milk:	0
protein (gm):	1.8	vegetable:	0
fat (gm):	0.7	fruit:	1
cholesterol (mg):	0	bread:	1
sodium (mg):	13	meat:	0
		fat:	0

Strawberries Romanoff

1 pint fresh strawberries, rinsed
  and halved, stems removed
3 tablespoons brandy

2 tablespoons Grand Marnier or
  other orange liqueur
1 teaspoon sunflower oil
1 tablespoon orange zest,
  grated
Nutmeg, pinch, grated
Serves 4.

Arrange strawberries in 4 champagne glasses; refrigerate.

Combine remaining ingredients in a small saucepan. Cook over medium heat till mixture starts to simmer, about 1 minute. Remove from heat and carefully ignite with a long match. Shake pan well till flames subside, then spoon 1 tablespoon of mixture over each portion of strawberries.

Note: It is not recommended that you freeze this dish.

Per Serving:		Diabetic Exchanges per Serving:	
calories:	81	milk:	0
protein (gm):	0.4	vegetable:	0
fat (gm):	1.4	fruit:	½
cholesterol (mg):	0	bread:	0
sodium (mg):	1	meat:	0
		fat:	1

Fruit Filling

1 container (8 ozs.) frozen light whipped topping, thawed

1 cup chopped cherries, blueberries, strawberries, peaches, etc.

Serves 4.

Mix topping with fruit in bowl. Add natural juice and mix well. Makes enough filling for two jelly-roll style cakes.

To Freeze: Vacuum seal each portion; label and freeze for up to 2 months.

To Serve: Thaw in refrigerator or in bowl of water. Serve chilled.

Per Serving:		Diabetic Exchanges per Serving:	
calories:	192	milk:	0
protein (gm):	0.9	vegetable:	0
fat (gm):	14.5	fruit:	1
cholesterol (mg):	0	bread:	0
sodium (mg):	14	meat:	0
		fat:	3

16
Sauces Sorcery

Chocolate Sauce I

2 tablespoons sugar
2 tablespoons unsweetened
cocoa

1 teaspoon cornstarch
½ cup water
½ teaspoon vanilla extract
Make ½ cup sauce.
Serves 4.

Combine all ingredients in small saucepan; bring to a boil over medium heat, stirring constantly. Boil mixture 1 minute, stirring constantly. Remove from heat and let sauce cool.

To Freeze: Place in microwave-safe casserole; label and freeze for up to 2 months.

To Serve: Thaw and serve cold, or reheat in microwave oven on High 2 to 3 minutes.

Per Serving:		Diabetic Exchanges per Serving:	
calories:	33	milk:	0
protein (gm):	0.7	vegetable:	0
fat (gm):	0.4	fruit:	0
cholesterol (mg):	0	bread:	½
sodium (mg):	2	meat:	0
		fat:	0

Chocolate Sauce II

1 teaspoon cornstarch
½ cup water
2 tablespoons unsweetened
  cocoa

3 tablespoons honey
½ teaspoon vanilla extract
Makes ½ cup sauce.
Serves 4.

Combine cornstarch and water in small saucepan; add remaining ingredients, stirring until smooth. Cook mixture over medium heat, until it begins to boil, about 1 minute, stirring constantly. Cover and chill.

To Freeze: Place in microwave-safe casserole; label and freeze for up to 2 months.

To Serve: Thaw and serve cold, or reheat in microwave on High 2 to 3 minutes.

Per Serving:		Diabetic Exchanges per Serving:	
calories:	59	milk:	0
protein (gm):	0.7	vegetable:	0
fat (gm):	0.4	fruit:	0
cholesterol (mg):	0	bread:	1
sodium (mg):	3	meat:	0
		fat:	0

Chocolate Sauce III

⅓ cup Dutch process cocoa
¼ cup firmly packed brown
   sugar

½ cup non-fat buttermilk
2 teaspoons crème de cacao
Makes ¾ cup.
Serves 6.

Combine cocoa and sugar in small saucepan. Gradually add buttermilk, stirring well. Place over medium heat and cook until sugar dissolves. Stir in liqueur; remove from heat.

To Freeze: Place in microwave-safe casserole; label and freeze for up to 2 months.

To Serve: Thaw and serve cold, or reheat in microwave on High 2 to 3 minutes.

Per Serving:		Diabetic Exchanges per Serving:	
calories:	65	milk:	0
protein (gm):	1.8	vegetable:	0
fat (gm):	0.8	fruit:	0
cholesterol (mg):	0	bread:	1
sodium (mg):	27	meat:	0
		fat:	0

Raspberry Sauce

1 package (10 oz.) frozen, unsweetened raspberries

1 tablespoon honey or granulated sugar

Serves 6.

In blender, process raspberries. Stir in honey or sugar.

To Freeze: Place in microwave-safe casserole; label and freeze for up to 2 months.

To Serve: Thaw and serve cold, or reheat in microwave oven on High 2 to 3 minutes.

Per Serving:		Diabetic Exchanges per Serving:	
calories:	34	milk:	0
protein (gm):	0.4	vegetable:	0
fat (gm):	0.2	fruit:	½
cholesterol (mg):	0	bread:	0
sodium (mg):	0	meat:	0
		fat:	0

Rum Raisin Sauce

¾ cup evaporated skim milk
1 tablespoon sugar
½ teaspoon cornstarch

¼ cup raisins
½ teaspoon vanilla extract
½ teaspoon rum extract
Makes ½ cup plus 2 tablespoons.
Serves 5.

Combine first 3 ingredients in small saucepan and place over medium heat; cook 10 minutes or until thickened, stirring frequently. Cook 1 minute more, then stir in raisins and vanilla. Remove from heat and stir in rum extract. Serve warm.

To Freeze: Place in microwave-safe casserole; label and freeze for up to 2 months.

To Serve: Thaw and serve cold, or reheat in microwave oven on High 2 to 3 minutes.

Per Serving:		Diabetic Exchanges per Serving:	
calories:	64	milk:	½
protein (gm):	3.1	vegetable:	0
fat (gm):	0.1	fruit:	½
cholesterol (mg):	1	bread:	0
sodium (mg):	44	meat:	0
		fat:	0

Mock Sour Cream

¼ to ½ cup buttermilk
½ teaspoon lemon juice
Makes 2 cups.
Serves 16.

1 cup low-fat cottage cheese

Place ingredients in blender and blend until smooth.

To Freeze: Place in microwave-safe casserole; label and freeze for up to 2 months.

To Serve: Thaw and serve cold, or reheat in microwave oven on High 2 to 3 minutes.

Per Serving:		Diabetic Exchanges per Serving:	
calories:	14	milk:	0
protein (gm):	2.0	vegetable:	0
fat (gm):	0.3	fruit:	0
cholesterol (mg):	1	bread:	0
sodium (mg):	61	meat:	0
		fat:	0

Cran-Orange Dip

½ cup cranberries, finely chopped

½ cup sugar-free orange marmalade
1 teaspoon orange juice
1 teaspoon orange rind

Makes ¾ cup.
Serves 6.

Combine all ingredients in small saucepan, and cook over medium heat until thoroughly heated. Serve "dip" warm.

To Freeze: Place in microwave-safe casserole; label and freeze for up to 2 months.

To Serve: Thaw and serve cold, or reheat in microwave oven on High 2 to 3 minutes.

Per Serving:		Diabetic Exchanges per Serving:	
calories:	37	milk:	0
protein (gm):	0.0	vegetable:	0
fat (gm):	0.0	fruit:	½
cholesterol (mg):	0	bread:	0
sodium (mg):	23	meat:	0
		fat:	0

Dill Sauce

2 cups plain low-fat yogurt
4 teaspoons dried dill weed
½ teaspoon Spike

Dill sprigs, fresh (garnish)
Makes 2 cups.
Serves 16.

Combine all ingredients, except fresh dill, and mix well. Cover tightly and store in refrigerator. Garnish with fresh dill before serving.

To Freeze: Place in microwave-safe casserole; label and freeze for up to 2 months.

To Serve: Thaw and serve cold, or reheat in microwave oven on High 2 to 3 minutes.

Per Serving:		Diabetic Exchanges per Serving:	
calories:	18	milk:	½
protein (gm):	1.3	vegetable:	0
fat (gm):	0.4	fruit:	0
cholesterol (mg):	1	bread:	0
sodium (mg):	18	meat:	0
		fat:	0

Lemon Wine Sauce for Fish

1 tablespoon cornstarch
1 cup Rhine or other dry
   white wine

1 ½ tablespoons diet margarine
2 tablespoons fresh lemon
   juice
1 lemon, sliced

Makes 1¼ cups sauce.
Serves 10.

Make a smooth paste of cornstarch and wine. Melt margarine in small saucepan. Add wine paste and cook, stirring constantly, until sauce is clear and slightly thickened. Add lemon juice and slices. Heat a few minutes longer and pour over baked, broiled, or poached fish.

To Freeze: Place in microwave-safe casserole; label and freeze for up to 2 months.

To Serve: Thaw and serve cold, or reheat in microwave on High 2 to 3 minutes.

Per Serving:		Diabetic Exchanges per Serving:	
calories:	27	milk:	0
protein (gm):	0.0	vegetable:	0
fat (gm):	0.8	fruit:	0
cholesterol (mg):	0	bread:	0
sodium (mg):	34	meat:	0
		fat:	½

Salsa

I think that once you serve fresh, homemade salsa you will never go back to buying bottled brands.

3 large vine-ripened tomatoes, seeded and chopped
¾ cup green onions, chopped

3 tablespoons green chilies, minced (use jalapeño if you want it hot)
1 tablespoon cilantro, minced
½ teaspoon celery seed
1 tablespoon red wine vinegar
Black pepper, freshly ground
Makes 2 + cups.
Serves 16.

Place all ingredients in bowl and mix well. Chill before serving.

To Freeze: Place in microwave-safe casserole; label and freeze for up to 2 months.

To Serve: Thaw and serve cold, or reheat in microwave oven on High 2 to 3 minutes.

Per Serving:		Diabetic Exchanges per Serving:	
calories:	6	milk:	0
protein (gm):	0.2	vegetable:	0
fat (gm):	0.0	fruit:	0
cholesterol (mg):	0	bread:	0
sodium (mg):	25	meat:	0
		fat:	0

Zesty Cocktail Sauce

¾ cup low-sodium dietetic catsup
2 tablespoons horseradish (to taste)
2 tablespoons lemon juice
¼ cup celery, finely chopped

1 tablespoon fresh basil, minced, or 2 teaspoons dried and crumbled
1 tablespoon fresh parsley, minced
1 teaspoon Worcestershire sauce
Tabasco, dash
Makes about 1 cup.
Serves 8.

Combine all ingredients in medium-size bowl. Mix well.

To Freeze: Place in microwave-safe casserole; label and freeze for up to 2 months.
To Serve: Thaw and serve cold, or reheat in microwave oven on High 2 to 3 minutes.

Per Serving:		Diabetic Exchanges per Serving:	
calories:	18	milk:	0
protein (gm):	0.4	vegetable:	0
fat (gm):	0.0	fruit:	0
cholesterol (mg):	0	bread:	0
sodium (mg):	195	meat:	0
		fat:	0

17
BEVERAGE DELIGHTS

Cran-Orange Tea

6 cups water
2 tea bags (any plain tea will do)
2 cups cranberry juice cocktail

2 cups orange juice
¼ cup sugar
2 tablespoons lemon juice
4 whole cloves
1 (3-in.) stick cinnamon
Crushed ice
Makes 2½ quarts.
Serves 12.

Bring water to boil; pour over tea bags. Cover and let stand 10 minutes. Discard tea bags. Combine tea and all other ingredients except ice in stockpot; simmer 10 minutes. (Do not boil.) Let stand to cool; cover and chill. Serve over crushed ice.

To Freeze: Place in quart containers; label and freeze for up to 3 months.

To Serve: Thaw and serve with ice.

Per Serving:		Diabetic Exchanges per Serving:	
calories:	57	milk:	0
protein (gm):	0.2	vegetable:	0
fat (gm):	0.0	fruit:	1
cholesterol (mg):	0	bread:	0
sodium (mg):	2	meat:	0
		fat:	0

Green Goblin Punch

6-oz. can frozen lemonade concentrate, thawed
2 cans (6 oz. each) frozen limeade concentrate, thawed

2 cups water
Few drops green food coloring
2 bottles (28 oz. each) ginger ale, chilled
Ice cubes or ice ring

Serves 22 (½-cup servings).

In large pitcher or punch bowl, combine concentrates and water. Add food coloring. Just before serving, add ginger ale and ice; stir to blend. Garnish as desired.

To Freeze: Place in quart containers; label and freeze for up to 3 months.

To Serve: Thaw and serve with ice.

Per Serving:		Diabetic Exchanges per Serving:	
calories:	55	milk:	0
protein (gm):	0.0	vegetable:	0
fat (gm):	0.0	fruit:	1
cholesterol (mg):	0	bread:	0
sodium (mg):	5	meat:	0
		fat:	0

Hot Mulled Cider

½ cup brown sugar
2 qts. cider

1 teaspoon whole allspice
1½ teaspoons whole cloves
2 cinnamon sticks
Orange slices
Makes about 8 cups.
Serves 16.

Put all ingredients in crockpot. If desired, tie whole spices in cheesecloth or put in tea strainer. Cover and cook on Low 2 to 8 hours. Serve from crockpot with ladle.

Note: If spices are added loose, strain before serving.

To Freeze: Place in quart containers; label and freeze for up to 3 months.

To Serve: Thaw and heat on top of stove till steaming.

Per Serving:		Diabetic Exchanges per Serving:	
calories:	31	milk:	0
protein (gm):	0.0	vegetable:	0
fat (gm):	0.0	fruit:	½
cholesterol (mg):	0	bread:	0
sodium (mg):	2	meat:	0
		fat:	0

Hot Spiced Wine

½ cup brown sugar
2 bottles (fifths) wine (sweet sherry, claret, or port)

1 teaspoon whole allspice
1½ teaspoons whole cloves
2 cinnamon sticks
Orange slices

Makes about 8 cups.
Serves 16.

Put all ingredients in crockpot. Cover and cook on Low 2 to 8 hours. Serve from crockpot with ladle.

To Freeze: Place in quart containers; label and freeze for up to 3 months.

To Serve: Thaw and reheat on top of stove till steaming.

Per Serving:		Diabetic Exchanges per Serving:	
calories:	23	milk:	0
protein (gm):	0.0	vegetable:	0
fat (gm):	0.0	fruit:	0
cholesterol (mg):	0	bread:	0
sodium (mg):	0	meat:	0
		fat:	½

Witches' Brew

This is a holiday brew good for Halloween, Thanksgiving, or Christmas.

4 cups red wine
3 cups orange juice
½ cup sugar
¼ cup lemon juice
4 whole cloves
1 cinnamon stick

Serves 15 (½-cup servings).

In large saucepan, combine all ingredients. Over low heat, bring just to simmering, stirring occasionally. (Do not boil.) Remove cloves and cinnamon. Serve hot.

To Freeze: Place in quart containers; label and freeze for up to 3 months.

To Serve: Thaw and heat on top of stove till steaming.

Per Serving:		**Diabetic Exchanges per Serving:**	
calories:	90	milk:	0
protein (gm):	0.5	vegetable:	0
fat (gm):	0.0	fruit:	1
cholesterol (mg):	0	bread:	0
sodium (mg):	41	meat:	0
		fat:	1

Sangria

1 bottle (750 ml) dry red or
  rose wine
2 cups carbonated water

2 oranges
2 lemons or limes
½ cup sugar or 4 packets
  Equal®
Serves 8 (6-oz. servings).

Chill, separately, wine and carbonated water. Cut one orange and
one lemon into slices. Squeeze juice from remaining fruits into a
pitcher; stir in sugar. Stir in wine; add carbonated water and fruit
slices. Serve in pitcher with wooden paddle for stirring.

To Freeze: Place in quart container, without fruit; label and freeze
for up to 3 months.

To Serve: Thaw and place in pitcher with fruit and ice.

Per Serving:		Diabetic Exchanges per Serving:	
calories:	94	milk:	0
protein (gm):	0.4	vegetable:	0
fat (gm):	0.0	fruit:	1
cholesterol (mg):	0	bread:	0
sodium (mg):	62	meat:	0
		fat:	1

Wassail
(with or without rum)

2 qts. apple juice or cider
1 pt. low-calorie cranberry juice
¾ cup sugar
1 teaspoon aromatic bitters

2 sticks cinnamon
1 teaspoon whole allspice
1 small orange, studded with
   whole cloves
1 cup rum (optional)
Makes about 12 cups.
Serves 12.

Put all ingredients in crockpot. Cover and cook on High 1 hour, then on Low 4 to 8 hours. Serve warm from crockpot.

To Freeze: Place in quart containers; label and freeze for up to 3 months.

To Serve: Thaw and reheat on top of stove till steaming.

Per Serving:		Diabetic Exchanges per Serving:	
calories:	190	milk:	0
protein (gm):	0.1	vegetable:	0
fat (gm):	0.2	fruit:	2
cholesterol (mg):	0	bread:	½
sodium (mg):	6	meat:	0
		fat:	1

Holiday Scents

I love to brew this before entertaining for the Holidays. The fragrance *is wonderful and everyone will enjoy it.*

Whole Allspice
Whole Cloves
Cinnamon Sticks
Dried Orange Peel

Use all ingredients in equal parts. Mix together and put 1 tablespoon in a small saucepan with 3 cups of water. Bring to boil and simmer. Divine!

18
BREAKFAST TREATS

It will be easier for you to stay on your diet program if you have breakfast because you will be less hungry during the day and won't be as tempted to grab doughnuts in the morning or candy bars in the afternoon. All the excuses in the world will not make up for the difference breakfast will make in your diet.

If you are short on time, consider the breakfast shake or muffins or a waffle you just put in the toaster. If your body rhythm wants breakfast later than most people, carry muffins with you so you can have one when you want it.

The following recipes include those that can be used for work mornings and a few for mornings when you can languish and enjoy breakfast. Be sure to pick a couple that you can live with so you won't be tempted to skip breakfast.

You will lose weight faster if you eat at least three times a day. This will help to regulate your blood sugar level and give you more energy all day long. Even if you are on a low-calorie diet, allow one-third of your daily calories for breakfast. It could mean the difference between diet success and failure.

Granola

Granola is good any time. You might try mixing it with dry cereal or sprinkling it on yogurt. I like to make it at home so I can control the amount of sweetener in it. It takes 2 minutes to mix and 15 minutes to cook.

2–3 cups rolled oats
1 cup wheat germ
½ cup raw sunflower seeds
¼ cup sesame seeds
2 tablespoons honey
2 tablespoons vegetable oil
2 tablespoons raisins
Serves 35.

Put all ingredients, except raisins, in large bowl. After mixing well, bake in roasting pan at 300° for 15 minutes. Every 5 minutes, open oven and stir granola thoroughly so all parts get brown and crisp. Cool; add scattering of raisins. Store in large jar or canister.

This will make a good breakfast-in-a-hurry with skim milk. Or stir 2 tablespoons of granola into a container of plain low-fat yogurt. You can even take granola with you to work and nibble on it dry.

To Freeze: Vacuum seal individual portions; label and freeze for up to 2 months.

To Serve: Defrost on counter.

Per Serving:		Diabetic Exchanges per Serving:	
calories:	84	milk:	0
protein (gm):	3.3	vegetable:	0
fat (gm):	3.4	fruit:	0
cholesterol (mg):	0	bread:	1
sodium (mg):	0	meat:	0
		fat:	½

Scrambled Eggs with Smoked Salmon

2 ozs. smoked salmon, sliced
1 (8-oz.) container Egg Beaters
4 tablespoons fresh dill, chopped

Pepper, freshly ground to taste
2 tablespoons diet margarine
¼ cup mushrooms, chopped
¼ cup onion, chopped
2 sprigs fresh dill to garnish
Serves 2.

Chop up half the salmon, reserving the rest for garnish. Put Egg Beaters, chopped dill, and chopped salmon in bowl. Season with pepper. Beat lightly with fork.

Melt margarine in non-stick skillet set over moderately low heat. When it begins to foam, add mushrooms and onion and cook till onion is limp. Add Egg Beaters and stir with spatula till set. Garnish with sprigs of dill and sliced salmon.

To Freeze: Place in microwave-safe casserole; label and freeze for up to 2 months.

To Serve: Cover casserole with microwave-safe plastic wrap, and microwave on High 3 to 5 minutes. Garnish with dill and sliced salmon.

Per Serving:		Diabetic Exchanges per Serving:	
calories:	198	milk:	0
protein (gm):	20.6	vegetable:	0
fat (gm):	11.1	fruit:	0
cholesterol (mg):	8	bread:	0
sodium (mg):	575	meat:	3
		fat:	1

Vegetable Cheese Omelet

1 tomato, chopped
½ cup mushrooms, chopped
¼ cup green pepper, chopped
½ cup onion, chopped

1 teaspoon Italian herbs
1 (8-oz.) container Egg Beaters or 6 egg whites
1 egg yolk
½ cup part-skim mozzarella cheese, shredded
Serves 2.

In a bowl, mix vegetables with Italian herbs for filling and set aside.

Beat eggs with fork until light and foamy. Place omelet pan over medium heat. Add vegetable spray to pan. Pour eggs in quickly. With one hand, move pan back and forth while stirring eggs in a circular motion with fork held in other hand. Do not scrape bottom of pan.

When omelet is almost cooked, add filling and cheese, then fold omelet over. When omelet is done, roll out onto a platter.

To Freeze: Place in microwave-safe casserole; label and freeze for up to 2 months.

To Serve: Thaw. Cover with microwave-safe plastic wrap, and cook on High 3 to 5 minutes.

Per Serving:		Diabetic Exchanges per Serving:	
calories:	306	milk:	0
protein (gm):	31.5	vegetable:	1
fat (gm):	16.1	fruit:	0
cholesterol (mg):	140	bread:	0
sodium (mg):	499	meat:	4
		fat:	1½

Whole-Wheat Pancakes

½ cup all-purpose flour
½ cup whole-wheat flour
1 teaspoon baking powder
¾ cup skim milk
2 tablespoons frozen apple juice concentrate, thawed and undiluted
1 ½ tablespoons vegetable oil
1 tablespoon brown sugar
2 egg whites, beaten
Vegetable cooking spray
Makes 16 (3-in.) pancakes.
Serves 4.

Combine all-purpose flour, whole-wheat flour, and baking powder in large bowl and stir well. Combine skim milk, thawed apple juice concentrate, vegetable oil, brown sugar, and egg whites. Add to flour mixture and stir well.

Spoon 2 tablespoons batter per pancake onto hot, non-stick griddle coated with cooking spray. Turn pancakes when tops are covered with bubbles and edges look cooked.

To Freeze: Place in microwave-safe casserole; label and freeze for up to 2 months.

To Serve: Thaw. Cover with microwave-safe plastic wrap, and cook on High 3 to 5 minutes.

Per Serving:		Diabetic Exchanges per Serving:	
calories:	201	milk:	0
protein (gm):	6.9	vegetable:	0
fat (gm):	5.6	fruit:	0
cholesterol (mg):	0	bread:	2
sodium (mg):	138	meat:	0
		fat:	1

Yogurt-Poppyseed Scones

2⅔ cups all-purpose flour
3 tablespoons sugar
1 teaspoon baking powder
6 tablespoons (¾ stick) chilled margarine, cut into small pieces

2 egg whites
1 egg, separated
1 cup plain yogurt
3 tablespoons poppyseed
1 tablespoon water
Makes 12 scones.
Serves 12.

Preheat oven to 400°. Spray a cookie sheet with non-stick vegetable spray.

Combine first 3 ingredients in large bowl. Using pastry blender or 2 knives, cut in margarine until mixture resembles coarse meal. Mix egg whites and yolk of separated egg. Stir into batter. Blend in yogurt and poppyseed. Mix well.

Turn mixture out onto lightly floured surface. Knead briefly until dough comes together. Roll out to thickness of 1 in. Cut into circles with 2-in. biscuit cutter or glass beaker. Gather scraps; reroll and cut additional scones. Place on prepared cookie sheet.

Mix remaining egg white with water. Brush tops of scones to glaze. Bake until golden brown, about 20 minutes. Serve immediately.

To Freeze: Vacuum seal individual scones; label and freeze for up to 1 month.

To Serve: Thaw on counter or in refrigerator. Warm in microwave if desired.

Per Serving:		Diabetic Exchanges per Serving:	
calories:	162	milk:	0
protein (gm):	5.1	vegetable:	0
fat (gm):	4.7	fruit:	0
cholesterol (mg):	18	bread:	1½
sodium (mg):	121	meat:	0
		fat:	1

Fruit-Filled Muffins

2 cups all-purpose flour
¼ cup granulated sugar
1 tablespoon baking powder
¼ teaspoon salt
1 large egg
1 cup plain yogurt or buttermilk

¼ cup (½ stick) diet margarine, melted
1 teaspoon vanilla extract
¼ cup fruit-only preserves (orange marmalade, strawberry, raspberry, and blueberry are especially good, but be inventive)

Makes 8 muffins.
Serves 8.

Heat oven to 375°. Grease 8 regular muffin cups or use foil baking cups.

Thoroughly mix flour, sugar, baking powder, and salt in large bowl. In smaller bowl, whisk egg with yogurt, margarine, and vanilla until smooth. Pour over flour mixture, folding in just until dry ingredients are moistened.

Spoon 1 heaping tablespoon of batter into each muffin cup. Make a small well in center of each, and fill with about 1 teaspoon of preserves. Top with about 2 more tablespoons batter to cover preserves.

Bake 25 to 30 minutes or until golden brown. Let cool about 5 minutes before removing from pans.

To Freeze: Vacuum seal individual muffins; label and freeze for up to 1 month.

To Serve: Thaw on counter or in refrigerator. Warm in microwave if desired.

Per Serving:		Diabetic Exchanges per Serving:	
calories:	195	milk:	0
protein (gm):	5.2	vegetable:	0
fat (gm):	4.1	fruit:	0
cholesterol (mg):	28	bread:	2
sodium (mg):	292	meat:	0
		fat:	1

Honey-Fruit Spread

Delicious on muffins, pancakes, or waffles.

6 ozs. plain low-fat yogurt
4 teaspoons honey
¼ cup strawberries, raspberries, or blueberries or just plain orange peel

Makes about 1 cup.
Serves 8.

Whip all ingredients together, using whisk till well blended. Refrigerate until ready to serve with muffins, pancakes, or waffles.

To Freeze: Vacuum seal; and freeze for up to 2 months.

To Serve: Defrost in refrigerator and serve.

Per Serving:		Diabetic Exchanges per Serving:	
calories:	25	milk:	0
protein (gm):	1.1	vegetable:	0
fat (gm):	0.3	fruit:	½
cholesterol (mg):	1	bread:	0
sodium (mg):	15	meat:	0
		fat:	0

Breakfast Shake

½ large (8–10 in.) banana,
   frozen
½ cup orange juice

½ cup skim milk
2 tablespoons wheat germ
½ teaspoon vanilla extract
1 teaspoon vegetable oil
2 ice cubes
Serves 1.

Peel banana, cut in half, and wrap halves separately in aluminum foil or other airtight wrapper to freeze overnight. The next day, combine all ingredients in blender or food processor. Cover and blend until smooth. Serve immediately.

Note: Do not freeze this recipe; make it fresh.

Per Serving:		Diabetic Exchanges per Serving:	
calories:	239	milk:	½
protein (gm):	8.8	vegetable:	0
fat (gm):	6.6	fruit:	2
cholesterol (mg):	2	bread:	½
sodium (mg):	68	meat:	0
		fat:	1

Sunshine Parfait

¾ cup plain non-fat yogurt
¼ teaspoon vanilla extract

½ cup strawberries, sliced
¼ cup blueberries
½ oz. granola
Serves 1.

In small bowl, combine yogurt and vanilla. In parfait glass, layer ¼ cup yogurt, strawberries, blueberries, and remaining yogurt. Top with granola.

To Freeze: I like to make these in Tupperware containers with lids. You can label and freeze them for up to 2 months.

To Serve: Thaw in refrigerator.

Per Serving:		Diabetic Exchanges per Serving:	
calories:	218	milk:	1
protein (gm):	11.0	vegetable:	0
fat (gm):	5.5	fruit:	1
cholesterol (mg):	10	bread:	½
sodium (mg):	152	meat:	0
		fat:	1

19
$\mathbf{P}$ARTY IN AN $\mathbf{H}$OUR

Today, you can enjoy effortless entertaining with a few timesavers. Select a menu rich in foods that need little cooking and can be made ahead. Choose dishes everyone loves, but add a few special touches to make them your own. Choose a centerpiece you can make in a few minutes, and set a table to complete the party theme. Anyone can become a great host or hostess; it just takes a little planning.

In this chapter you will be introduced to party themes that you can put together in an hour. We will cover the food, beverages, and centerpieces so you will be ready to welcome your guests with little effort. You will find menus for each of the parties, and the *recipes for all the food are included in the book (see Index),* with the exception of breads and salads. You will notice a reference to "Great Green Salad." That is my term for any green salad you like to prepare and is quick to make.

Buffet
Party

Antipasto
Fettuccine with Asparagus and
Shrimp in Parmesan Sauce

Italian Bread
Light Poundcake with Rum Raisin Sauce
Wine, Coffee
Serves 8.

1 Hour Before Serving:
1. Steam asparagus unless using canned, and set aside.
2. Assemble Antipasto and refrigerate.
3. Boil water for pasta; meanwhile prepare pasta sauce.
4. Put food on buffet; uncork wine.
5. Prepare coffee and Rum Raisin Sauce.
6. Slice cake on platter. Spoon sauce over cake and serve with coffee.

Centerpiece:
A large bowl of whole vegetables with some dried flowers tucked in.

Outdoor Concert Dinner

Chilled Champagne with Fresh Strawberries

Raw Vegetables and Mediterranean Artichoke Dip
Pasta Niçoise (double batch)
Great Green Salad
Peaches Amaretto
Peach-Flavored Coffee
Serves 8.

1 Hour Before Leaving for Concert:
1. Prepare Artichoke Dip and refrigerate.
2. Boil water for pasta and cook pasta; drain and set aside.
3. Chop vegetables for dip.
4. Assemble Pasta Niçoise. Start brewing coffee.
5. Make Pasta Niçoise dressing and store in plastic container.
6. Make salad dressing and pack in separate plastic containers. (Mark each one.)
7. Place veggies for dip in a basket and cover with plastic wrap.
8. Prepare Peaches Amaretto, but pack cookies or granola separately so you can add them later.
9. Pack strawberries for champagne. Put coffee in Thermos.

At the Concert:
1. Prepare a glass of champagne for each guest.
2. Serve vegetables and dip.
3. Pour dressing over pasta and serve.
4. Pour dressing over salad and serve.
5. Add cookie or granola topping to peaches and serve.

Centerpiece:
A bowl of strawberries, with stems, to be dunked in the champagne.

Halloween In the Family Room

Salmon Ball
Carrot Soup with Dill

Poached Turkey Breast with Herbs and Wine
Great Green Salad
Angel Food Cake (purchased) with Raspberry Sauce
Witches' Brew, Green Goblin Punch
Serves 6.

1 Hour Before Serving:
1. Prepare Witches' Brew and put on stove to simmer.
2. Prepare Green Goblin Punch and refrigerate.
3. Cook carrots for soup. Meanwhile, while carrots are cooking, prepare Turkey Breast.
4. Prepare Salmon Ball and place on buffet. Finish soup. Keep warm.
5. Prepare Great Green Salad.
6. Prepare Raspberry Sauce and set aside.
7. While guests are enjoying the Salmon Ball, scoop out pumpkin and pour in the soup.
8. Serve soup.
9. Serve Turkey Breast and salad.

At the Table:
Cut the store-bought Angel Food Cake and pour Raspberry Sauce on each piece.

Centerpiece:
A large tray decorated with autumn leaves, gourds, and a pumpkin in the center. For this party, the pumpkin in the centerpiece becomes the tureen for the soup.

Tree- Trimming Party

Spicy Popcorn Schnibble
Marinated Mushroons
Pasta with Porcini Mushroom
Sauce

French Bread
Great Green Salad
Fresh Fruit Salad with Grand Marnier
Hot Mulled Cider, Beer, Wine
Serves 6.

Morning of the Party:
1. Prepare Hot Mulled Cider.
2. Get cut up fruit from salad bar of your supermarket.

1 Hour Before Serving:
1. Prepare Spicy Popcorn Schnibble and set on buffet.
2. Prepare Marinated Mushrooms and set on buffet.
3. Put Hot Mulled Cider on buffet, and offer appetizers to tree trimmers.
4. Prepare pasta sauce and keep warm. Slice bread. Prepare salad.
5. Boil water for pasta while you make salad. Cook pasta.

At the Table:
1. Pour dressing over salad and serve.
2. Serve pasta and Parmesan cheese.
3. Complete and serve dessert.

Centerpiece:
A natural wicker basket filled with holly and pine cones and decorated with a holiday bow.

Super Bowl Party

Mexican Popcorn
Salmon Ball with Cucumbers
and Celery

Great Green Salad
Speedy Chili
Corn Bread (purchased)
Football Cake
Beer, Wine, Cider, Coffee
Serves 8.

Day of the Party:
1. *First Quarter*—Prepare Cake and place in oven. Prepare Chili and place on medium heat. Prepare and serve Popcorn and beer.
2. *Second Quarter*—Prepare and serve Salmon Ball.
3. *Third Quarter*—Prepare and toss salad. Slice bread. Place chili in serving bowl and serve.
4. *Fourth Quarter*—Prepare coffee and beverages. Complete Cake and serve.

Centerpiece:
Store-bought pot of mums arranged in a basket.

Valentine's Day

Shrimp with Zesty Cocktail Sauce
Cioppino

French Bread
Chocolate Hearts with Assorted Berries
Wine, Coffee
Serves 6.

Morning of the Party:
1. Prepare Cioppino and place stockpot on medium heat. Set timer for 1 hour.
2. Prepare Chocolate Sponge Cake and place in oven to bake.
3. Prepare Cocktail Sauce and refrigerate until ready to use.
4. Combine berries with sugar, mix well, and refrigerate.
5. Cut hearts from cake and set aside. Make chocolate sauce.

At the Table:
1. Assemble Shrimp Cocktail and serve.
2. Put Cioppino in tureen and serve with bread.
3. Prepare coffee.
4. Assemble dessert and serve with coffee.

Centerpiece:
Store-bought rosebuds with baby's breath in a small vase with candles on each side.

Romantic Dinner for Two

Gazpacho
Great Green Salad

Crabmeat-Topped Baked Potatoes
Filet of Sole Veracruzana
Strawberries Romanoff
White Wine, Coffee
Serves 2.

Morning of the Dinner:
1. Rinse berries and refrigerate.

1 Hour Before Serving:
1. Prepare Gazpacho and refrigerate.
2. Prepare salad and refrigerate.
3. Bake potatoes in microwave and set aside. Prepare crabmeat topping.
4. Prepare fish and microwave. Add potatoes 2 minutes before fish is done.

At the Table:
1. Light candles. Serve wine.
2. Serve Gazpacho.
3. Serve salad, fish, and potatoes with topping.
4. Prepare coffee while you complete dessert.
5. Serve dessert and coffee.

Centerpiece:
A green plant with 3 fresh roses, carnations, or daisies placed in the center. Light 2 candles that match the color of the flowers.

INDEX

The Restaurant Companion: A Guide to Healthier Eating Out by Hope Warshaw, M.M.Sc., R.D.

All the practical information you need to order low-fat, high-nutrition meals in 15 popular cuisines! At Chinese, Italian, or Mexican restaurants, fast-food chains, salad bars—even on airlines—you'll learn how to stay in control of calories, fat, sodium, and cholesterol when eating out.

Skinny Spices by Erica Levy Klein

50 nifty homemade spice blends, ranging from Ha Cha chili to Moroccan mint, to make even diet meals exciting! Spice blends require no cooking and add *zero* fat, cholesterol, or calories to food. Includes 100 recipes that use the blends.

The Love Your Heart Low Cholesterol Cookbook by Carole Kruppa

Give your taste buds a treat and your heart a break with 250 low-cholesterol recipes for everything from appetizers to desserts. Enjoy the great tastes—with *no* cholesterol—of deviled eggs, Italian bean soup, oriental chicken salad, chocolate cake, and many more easy-to-make delights. Nutritional data, diabetic exchanges, and calorie counts.

Feeding Your Baby: From Conception to Age 2 by Louise Lambert-Lagacé

First U.S. edition. Complete information on good nutrition for babies—and mothers—before, during, and after pregnancy. Includes breast-feeding (with tips for working moms), advice on formulas, how to introduce solids, recipes for homemade baby foods, dealing with problem eaters, and much more. Extensive nutritional information in plain talk.